4 Practice Tests for the

TOEFL®

2019–2020

Special thanks to the team who made this book possible:

Sumi Aktar, Kim Bowers, Matthew Callan, Louise Cook, Scarlet Edmonds, Joanna Graham, Brian Holmes, Nimesh Shah

TOEFL iBT® is a registered trademark of the Educational Testing Service, which neither sponsors nor endorses this product.

Published by Kaplan Publishing, a division of Kaplan, Inc.
750 Third Avenue
New York, NY 10017

10 9 8 7 6 5 4 3 2 1

ISBN: 978-1-5062-3738-1

TABLE OF CONTENTS

How To Use This Book

WELCOME TO KAPLAN TOEFL PRACTICE TESTS

Congratulations on your decision to improve your English proficiency, and thank you for choosing Kaplan for your TOEFL preparation. You've made the right choice in acquiring this book—you're now armed with four full length TOEFL practice tests, produced as a result of decades of researching the TOEFL and similar tests and teaching many thousands of students the skills they need to succeed.

This book is guaranteed to help you to score higher—let's start by walking through what you need to know to take advantage of this book and the Audio Tracks.

Your Book

This book contains four TOEFL practice tests, which include full-length Listening, Reading, Writing and Speaking subtests. To listen to the audio for the practice tests in this book, first register by visiting **www.kaptest.com/booksonline**. You can then listen to the audio online on your computer, or on your device through the Kaplan Study App, which can be downloaded in the App Store from your iOS device or the Google Play Store from your Android device.

Review the listening scripts and answers at the back of this book to better understand your performance. Look for patterns in the questions you answered correctly and incorrectly. Were you stronger in some areas than others? This analysis will help you to target specific areas when you practice and prepare for the TOEFL.

Practice
Test 1

TEST DIRECTIONS

This test is designed to measure your ability to understand and to use English in an academic context. The test has four sections.

In the **Reading** section, you will read three passages and answer questions about them.

In the **Listening** section, you will listen to two dialogues and four talks and answer questions about them.

In the **Speaking** section, there are six tasks. The first two tasks ask you to speak based on your own personal experience. In the other four, you will read passages and/or listen to dialogues and talks, then speak based on what you have read and/or heard.

In the **Writing** section, there are two tasks. In the first task, you will read a passage, listen to a talk, then write based on what you have read and heard. The second task asks you to write based on your own personal experience and ideas.

There is a 10-minute break after the **Listening** section.

At the beginning of each section, there are directions that explain how to answer the questions or respond to the tasks in the section.

In the **Reading** and **Listening** sections, you should work carefully but quickly. You should try to answer every question to the best of your ability. Make an educated guess on questions that you are unsure of. In the **Speaking** and **Writing** sections, each task is separately timed. In each case, you should try to respond to the task as completely as possible in the given time.

READING SECTION

Directions: In this section of the test, you will read three passages. You will be tested on your ability to understand them by answering several questions on each passage.

While you read, you may take notes. You can then use your notes when answering questions.

Most questions are worth one point. Questions that are worth more than one point have a special note telling you how many total points they are worth.

You will have 60 minutes to read the three passages and answer all the questions. If you finish the questions before 60 minutes is up, you can go back and review your work in this section.

Passage 1

Nathaniel Hawthorne: His Life and Work

Nathaniel Hawthorne was born on the United States' birthday, July 4th, in 1804 to a prominent colonial family in Salem, Massachusetts. Hawthorne deliberately set out to create an American voice in literature. Believing that American authors of his time were mimicking the style of the British Romantics, Hawthorne refused to imitate others and developed a new style of writing using distinctly American themes and settings.

Hawthorne's most critically acclaimed and popular novel was *The Scarlet Letter*, but his body of work reaches far beyond this classic to include children's books, essays, short stories, and a comedy. Hawthorne often complained that America lacked literary subject matter equal to Europe's, which had inspired its Romantics. In his personal life and family history, however, Hawthorne did find a deep well of inspiration. Many critics have suggested that Hawthorne's central concern, the dark side of morality, was informed by a sense of guilt over the roles his ancestors had played in early America. He was a descendant of John Hawthorne, one of the infamous judges of the Salem witchcraft trials of 1692. His family had also participated in the persecution of the Quakers earlier in the 17th century.

His time at Bowdoin College in Maine (1821–1825) proved to have great significance in his life, for he formed lifelong political and literary friends there. Those years provided subject matter for his first novel, *Fanshawe*, which he published at his own expense in 1828. (Legend holds that the author, ashamed of the work, burned the unsold copies.) While Hawthorne did not believe that his writing had yet achieved eloquence, his experiences at Bowdoin brought him into companionship with such men as Henry Wadsworth Longfellow, Horatio Bridge, and Franklin Pierce, who would become the 14th president of the United States. After college, Hawthorne dabbled briefly in the transcendentalist movement, an experience that would give him a taste of communal living and inspire the setting for *The Blithedale Romance*, written in 1852. It was around this time that Hawthorne befriended and won the respect of Herman Melville, who would later dedicate *Moby-Dick* to him.

A Hawthorne next tried his hand at children's books: *Grandfather's Chair* (1841), *Famous Old People* (1841), *Liberty Tree* (1841), and *Biographical Stories for Children* (1842) were little known but critically acclaimed. **B** It was not until the publishing of his story of the victims of Puritan obsession and intolerance, *The Scarlet Letter*, that

Hawthorne reached his greatest renown. **C** The book is credited with influencing Henry James's *The Portrait of a Lady,* Kate Chopin's *The Awakening,* and William Faulkner's *As I Lay Dying.* **D** In Hawthorne's own words, "*The Scarlet Letter* is positively a hellfired story, into which I found it almost impossible to throw any cheering light."

The House of the Seven Gables, published the following year in 1851, was a farcical tale in which Hawthorne attempted to shine a redemptive light on some of the dark themes of *The Scarlet Letter.* Also based in Puritan New England, this book is considered a refutation of the notions of sin, the anguish wrought by guilt, and the lack of confession or forgiveness found in The Scarlet Letter. Rather, this light comedy has a theme of redemption* and features the Pynchon and Maule families overcoming sin and its consequences through renewal. In The House of the Seven Gables, Hawthorne conveys hope for the human cycle of sin, repentance, forgiveness, and restoration.

There is much legend attached to Hawthorne's life. Some reports characterize him as a brooding recluse who seldom went out. In fact, he was more social and urbane than is often assumed. Hawthorne married Sophia Amelia Peabody of Salem in 1842, and the couple settled in Concord, Massachusetts, in his mother's family home, referred to as the "Old Manse." When unable to provide for his family through his writing, he always took other work while continuing to write. Many of these positions were in government service, including an appointment from President Franklin Pierce, his old college friend, as consul in Liverpool, England. It was in Europe in 1860 that Hawthorne wrote his last novel, The Marble Faun, again taking up the subject of sin and guilt.

Hawthorne is considered the first American novelist to create dynamic characters with hidden motivations. Through symbolism, allegory, and character development, Hawthorne gave his readers psychological insight into the minds of the prideful, the secretive, and the guilty. In the process, he added to the respect given to American literature from the Old World.

*redemption: the act of being saved from the power of evil and its consequences

1   The word mimicking in the passage is closest in meaning to

   (A) mocking.
   (B) ignoring.
   (C) disputing.
   (D) copying.

2   According to the passage, Hawthorne published all of the following EXCEPT

   (A) poetry.
   (B) novels.
   (C) expository writing.
   (D) humorous works.

3 Which of the following sentences most closely expresses the important information in the highlighted sentence in the passage?

(A) Hawthorne's obsession with morality and sin certainly came from a sense of guilt over his family's ignoble history.

(B) Many critics believe that Hawthorne learned about issues of sin and morality from his ancestors, who played a prominent role in New England history.

(C) For some scholars, the guilt Hawthorne felt over the role his ancestors played in some of the darker chapters in American history explains the author's focus on sin and morality.

(D) Numerous critics have argued that Hawthorne's central concern with his ancestors' shameful deeds comes from the writer's deeply conflicted moralistic nature.

4 According to the passage, Hawthorne's family

(A) objected to his choice of career.

(B) had a long history in New England.

(C) was puritanical and conservative.

(D) was known for its wealth.

5 It can be inferred from the passage that Herman Melville was a

(A) famous politician.

(B) writer.

(C) transcendentalist.

(D) professor.

6 The word renown in paragraph 4 is closest in meaning to

(A) fame.

(B) respect.

(C) knowledge.

(D) wealth.

7 Look at the four letters (**A**, **B**, **C**, and **D**) in the passage that show where the following sentence could be inserted into the passage.

The title of the book refers to the letter A, a shameful symbol that women accused of adultery were forced to wear in Puritan New England.

Where would the sentence best fit in the passage? Choose the letter for the square where this sentence should be added.

8   Which novel of Hawthorne's is noted for its comparatively lighthearted tone?

(A) The Scarlet Letter

(B) Biographical Stories for Children

(C) The House of the Seven Gables

(D) Fanshawe

9   Contrary to what might be assumed about his personality, Hawthorne was

(A) someone who rarely went out.

(B) engaged in society and sophisticated activities.

(C) involved in local and international politics.

(D) known to be fond of parties.

10   It can be inferred from the passage that Hawthorne's writing

(A) made him very wealthy.

(B) did not make him rich.

(C) was his sole source of income.

(D) earned him almost no money in his lifetime.

11   Which of the following statements probably reflects the author's opinion of Nathaniel Hawthorne?

(A) Hawthorne contributed greatly to American literature.

(B) Most of Hawthorne's writing after The Scarlet Letter was a disappointment.

(C) Hawthorne's success was mainly due to his family's background.

(D) Hawthorne's importance to American literature has not been realized.

12   According to the passage, the most common theme in Hawthorne's work is

(A) transcendentalism.

(B) persecution.

(C) sin and guilt.

(D) forgiveness.

13 **Directions:** Find the phrases in the answer choices list that relate to the Hawthorne novel listed. Write your answers in the appropriate place. TWO of the answer choices will NOT match either category. This question is worth 4 points.

Answer Choices	*The Scarlet Letter*
A. Puritan morality without redemption	
B. Hope for the human condition	
C. Hawthorne's most famous work	
D. Published in 1842	*The House of the Seven Gables*
E. The Pynchon and Maule families	
F. Marital infidelity	
G. Dark themes lightened with humor	
H. Influenced other well-known authors	
I. Little known but critically acclaimed	

Passage 2

The Biological Effects of Ionizing Radiation

Energy transported by electromagnetic waves or by atomic particles is called radiation*. Our bodies are continuously bombarded with radiation from many directions. Radiation sources include: infrared, ultraviolet, and visible radiation from the sun; radio waves from radio and television stations; microwaves from microwave ovens; and x-rays from various medical procedures. In addition, natural and man-made radioactive materials are present in the soil and in many building materials.

When radiation is absorbed by biological systems, a number of things may happen. Electrons in the material may remain in the parent atom but be promoted to higher energy states. Molecules absorbing this radiation may increase their vibration, also called their rotation energies. Another possibility is that the radiation carries enough energy to break chemical bonds and remove an electron from the parent atom or molecule, forming an ion. This process is called ionization. In general, radiation that causes ionization (ionizing radiation) is far more harmful to biological systems than radiation that does not cause ionization (nonionizing radiation). Ionizing radiation cannot be detected with any of the five senses.

Most living tissue contains at least 70 percent water by mass. The chemistry of radiation is primarily due to the effects of ionizing radiation on water. It is common to define ionizing radiation as radiation that can ionize water, a process requiring a minimum energy of 1216 kilojoules per mole (18 grams) of water. Most alpha, beta, and gamma rays (as well as higher-energy ultraviolet rays) possess sufficient energies to ionize water. As ionizing radiation passes through living tissue, it removes electrons and forms highly reactive H2O+ ions. These charged ions can react with other water molecules to form H3O+ ions and a neutral but highly unstable and reactive OH (oxygen-hydrogen) molecule. This OH molecule is an example of a free radical, a substance with one or more unpaired electrons. In cells and tissues, free radicals can attack various biomolecules to form other free radicals, which, in turn, can attack other compounds. Thus, formation of a single free radical can initiate a large number of chemical reactions that are ultimately able to disrupt the normal operation of cells.

A The damage to cells produced by radiation depends on the length of time that the body is exposed and the energy of the radiation. **B** Biological effects are also influenced by the type of radiation and the location of the radiation in relation to the body. **C** The primary types of ionizing radiation—alpha particles, beta particles, and gamma rays—are most commonly found in radioactive and medical waste and certain natural elements, including uranium. **D**

Gamma rays are particularly harmful because they penetrate human tissue very easily. Consequently, the damage that they cause is not limited to the skin. The skin surface usually acts as a barrier to radiation from outside the body and stops most alpha particles. Beta particles are only able to penetrate about one centimeter beneath the skin surface. Hence, alpha and beta particles are not as dangerous as gamma rays unless the radiation source somehow enters the body. Ingestion of certain radioactive substances such as radon or plutonium can be very dangerous because these substances' chemical nature causes them to concentrate in the body organs or the bones and produce intense localized damage to the surrounding tissue.

In general, the tissues that show the greatest damage from radiation are those that reproduce rapidly, such as bone marrow, blood-forming tissues, and lymph nodes. The principal effect of extended exposure to low doses of radiation is an onset of cancer, which is an uncontrolled reproduction of cells due to damage to the cells' growth-regulation mechanism. Leukemia, characterized by excessive growth of white blood cells, is one of the major cancer problems associated with radiation.

radiation: a type of energy radiated or transmitted in the form of rays, waves, or particles

14 The words bombarded with in paragraph 1 are closest in meaning to

(A) shocked by.

(B) hit with.

(C) invaded by.

(D) filled with.

15 According to the passage, all of the following are sources of radiation EXCEPT

    (A) ultraviolet rays from the sun.

    (B) microwave ovens.

    (C) radioactive elements in the soil.

    (D) fluorescent lights.

16 All of the following are true about ionizing radiation EXCEPT

    (A) it can sometimes be smelled.

    (B) it is more dangerous than non-ionizing radiation.

    (C) it can result in the production of free radicals.

    (D) it can cause cancer.

17 The author discusses ionizing radiation in paragraph 3 in order to

    (A) explain its effects in comparison to non-ionizing radiation.

    (B) provide a scientific description of the process.

    (C) give examples of its negative health consequences.

    (D) emphasize the role water plays in its creation.

18 Based on information in paragraph 3, which of the following best explains the term free radical?

    (A) a potentially harmful molecule that is a by-product of radiation

    (B) a charged atom that reproduces biomolecules rapidly

    (C) an H_3O^+ ion formed as a consequence of ionizing radiation

    (D) a neutral but highly stable and reactive molecule

19 Which of the following sentences most closely expresses the important information in the highlighted sentence in the passage?

    (A) Just one free radical can thus be the impetus for a chemical process that may eventually lead to cellular damage.

    (B) In this way, a single free radical will ultimately disrupt the chemical structure and normal behavior of cells.

    (C) Nevertheless, the normal operation of cells can, in time, be negatively affected due to the chemical process that one free radical can begin.

    (D) Hence, free radicals can eventually disturb the normal activity of cells, unless the radiation victim is given chemical treatment.

20 Look at the four letters (**A**, **B**, **C**, and **D**) in the passage that show where the following sentence could be inserted into the passage.

X-rays, another potential source of ionizing radiation, are emitted by medical scanning devices, and, in much smaller quantities, by the cathode tubes in television screens and computer monitors.

Where would the sentence best fit in the passage? Choose the letter for the square where this sentence should be added.

21 The word penetrate in paragraph 5 is closest in meaning to

(A) scar.

(B) impale.

(C) puncture.

(D) enter.

22 It can be inferred from the passage that exposure to radiation

(A) almost always is fatal.

(B) usually leads to cancer.

(C) is generally unavoidable.

(D) is mostly harmless.

23 According to the passage, ionizing radiation is considered particularly dangerous primarily because

(A) it cannot be detected by the five senses.

(B) it can lead to uncontrolled cell reproduction.

(C) it increases cell rotation energy.

(D) it can penetrate the skin and damage organs.

24 According to the passage, which source of ionizing radiation is potentially harmful, even in small doses?

(A) the sun

(B) building materials

(C) radon

(D) radio waves

25 Directions: Below is an introductory sentence for a short summary of the passage. Complete the summary by choosing the THREE answer choices that express key ideas in the passage. Sentences that express ideas that are NOT in the passage or mention minor details do NOT belong in the summary. *This question is worth 2 points.*

Though we are surrounded by many forms of radiation, it is ionizing radiation that poses the greatest health risks.

Answer Choices	
A. The ionization of water produces free radicals that can destroy the normal operation of cells.	D. The harm caused by ionizing radiation depends on the nature of the exposure and the type of radiation.
B. Ionized water molecules can produce H3O+ ions and OH molecules, which are known as free radicals.	E. Although ionizing radiation is present in small quantities in everyday life, if not ingested, its potential for harm is negligible.
C. The primary adverse effect of extended exposure to ionizing radiation is cancer.	F. The most harmful rays can penetrate matter easily, including human tissue.

Passage 3

The Social Cognitive Theory of Learning

Learning is an important aspect of virtually all areas of life. From infancy through old age people must learn to talk, read, play, work, and get along socially in society. Due to its pervasive nature, learning has long been a topic of intense study within psychology. While psychologists tend to agree that learning plays a vital role in human functioning, they have developed very different perspectives, or theories, on its causes, processes, and consequences.

The learning theories that dominated the first half of the 20th century came predominantly from the behavioral school of psychology. Behaviorists view learning as a function of environmental factors that promote associations between stimuli and responses. Drawing on the animal experiments of Pavlov, who showed how dogs could learn to associate the sound of a bell with food, early behaviorists saw learning as a product of conditioning—that is—the repeated performance of an act, usually in the interest of some external reward. From the behavioral perspective, learning is essentially the repetition of externally reinforced behaviors.

Alfred Bandura began his research on observational learning in the early 1960s as a reaction to the behaviorist viewpoint on learning. The early research findings of Bandura and his colleagues challenged the prevailing view of learning by demonstrating that it is not necessary to perform a behavior in order to learn the behavior and that reinforcement is not a necessary component of learning. Social cognitive theory was developed by Bandura in order to provide a comprehensive explanation of observational learning.

Bandura's social cognitive theory is based on the assumption that the majority of learning done by humans occurs within a social environment. Modeling is a major construct of the theory and refers to the fact that people learn by observing the behavior of others and the response that the behaviors elicit from those around them. When people observe the consequences of modeled behaviors they gain information regarding the appropriateness of these behaviors. Research on modeling has been used to explain how people learn a variety of skills, beliefs, strategies, and knowledge.

The three functions of modeling proposed by Bandura's social cognitive theory are response facilitation, inhibition/disinhibition, and observational learning. Response facilitation involves the modeling of socially acceptable behavior. The modeled behavior tends to include social prompts that motivate the observer to perform the modeled behavior. Inhibition/disinhibition involves the modeling of socially unacceptable behavior. During inhibition the model receives punishment as a consequence for performing a prohibited behavior and the observer is discouraged from performing the behavior. On the other hand, during disinhibition the prohibited behavior being modeled does not result in a negative consequence for the model, and the observer is encouraged to perform the unacceptable behavior. Observational learning occurs when an observer performs a new behavior that they would not have performed prior to observing the behavior modeled.

The four sub processes involved in observational learning are attention, retention, production, and motivation. In order for observational learning to occur a person must be exposed to the behaviors of models within their daily lives and be capable of and willing to pay attention to these behaviors. **A** The specific characteristics of the model will influence how effective a model is at attracting attention. **B** People tend to attend to models that they regard as similar to themselves, models that they view as having power and status, and models that they view as kind and nurturing. **C** Features of the task being modeled are another variable that influences attention. **D** Thus teachers will often use bright colors, music, or odd shapes to encourage children to attend to their lessons.

Once the behavior of a model is observed the input received must be cognitively processed and retained in the form of a general rule. This general rule undergoes constant revision based on future observations of others as well as the input received from others regarding the performer's behavior. Production occurs when the observer translates the modeled behavior into overt behavior and performs the new behavior. Another sub process, motivation, plays an important role in production; behaviors viewed as important, ethical, or advantageous to the observer are the ones most often produced.

Bandura's research marked the beginning of a movement toward a view of learning that emphasizes cognitive rather than behavioral processes. Social cognitive theory has become one of the major cognitive learning theories dominating the psychological field today.

26 The phrase get along in paragraph 1 is closest in meaning to

- Ⓐ travel.
- Ⓑ succeed.
- Ⓒ cooperate.
- Ⓓ be healthy.

27 Based on the information in paragraph 1, which of the following best defines the term theories?

- Ⓐ sets of ideas that try to explain something about life or the world
- Ⓑ experiments that scientists carry out to determine if their ideas are true or false
- Ⓒ treatments that are intended to help people with learning disabilities
- Ⓓ types of psychological therapy that have not been proven to be helpful

28 Which idea is associated with stimulus/response?

- Ⓐ modeling
- Ⓑ behaviorism
- Ⓒ social cognitive theory
- Ⓓ observational learning

29 Which of the following sentences most closely expresses the important information in the highlighted sentence in the passage?

- Ⓐ Likewise, disinhibition involves the encouragement of behavior that is not socially acceptable.
- Ⓑ Disinhibition, however, occurs when the model receives a negative reaction for performing an act of conformity.
- Ⓒ Conversely, through the process of disinhibition, a behavior that is not considered socially acceptable can be encouraged.
- Ⓓ At the same time, if an observer is rewarded for an illicit behavior, which is known as disinhibition, he/she will not necessarily learn the behavior.

30 According to the information in paragraph 5, all of the following are aspects of the modeling component of the social cognitive theory EXCEPT

- Ⓐ the promotion of actions that society approves of.
- Ⓑ the discouragement of actions that society frowns upon.
- Ⓒ the acquisition of new behaviors.
- Ⓓ the repeated performance of a behavior.

31 Based on the information in paragraph 5, which of the following would most likely be considered an example of disinhibition?

- Ⓐ a teenager taking drugs at a party
- Ⓑ a child saying thank you for a gift
- Ⓒ a person receiving a speeding ticket
- Ⓓ a boy imitating the way his father talks

32 According to the information in paragraph 6, which is a necessary condition for observational learning to take place?

- Ⓐ Learners must witness the model's behavior on a regular basis.
- Ⓑ Learners must see the models as similar to themselves.
- Ⓒ Learners must be rewarded for paying attention to the model.
- Ⓓ Learners must regard the model as kind and nonthreatening.

33 Look at the four letters (**A**, **B**, **C**, and **D**) in the passage that show where the following sentence could be inserted.

It is therefore not surprising that for children, parents are among the earliest and most important models.

Where would the sentence best fit in the passage? Choose the letter for the square where this sentence should be added.

34 The author describes teachers' lessons in paragraph 6 in order to

- Ⓐ demonstrate the production sub process of observational learning.
- Ⓑ show how presentation can be used to promote attention.
- Ⓒ provide an example of modeling a person with power or status.
- Ⓓ refute the behavioral view of learning.

35 The word overt in the passage is closest in meaning to

- Ⓐ noticeable.
- Ⓑ prohibited.
- Ⓒ cognitive.
- Ⓓ proper.

36 According to the passage, how does motivation influence the production of learned behavior?

    (A) Only behaviors considered of benefit to the model will be produced.

    (B) Behaviors will only be produced when the learner believes he/she will receive a physical reward.

    (C) Motivation plays a small role in determining what behaviors will be produced.

    (D) Observers are more likely to produce behaviors that satisfy personal goals or moral standards.

37 According to the passage, the main difference between the behavioral and social cognitive theories is

    (A) the social cognitive theory maintains that learning can occur without the performance of a behavior.

    (B) the behavioral theory posits that learning is essentially a mental process.

    (C) the social cognitive theory holds that learning is a function of conditioned responses to environmental conditions.

    (D) the behavioral theory is no longer believed to provide an adequate explanation for human learning.

38 **Directions:** Below is an introductory sentence for a short summary of the passage. Complete the summary by choosing the THREE answer choices that express key ideas in the passage. Sentences that express ideas that are NOT in the passage or mention minor details do NOT belong in the summary. *This question is worth 2 points.*

Much research into the psychology of learning today is guided by social cognitive theory.

Answer Choices	
A. The social cognitive theory maintains that a great deal of human learning occurs through modeling, of which observational learning is an important part.	D. Early behavioral theory was based on the canine experiments of Pavlov, who found the ringing of a bell could be associated with food.
B. Alfred Bandura proposed the social cognitive theory based on research that found a great deal of learning occurs through observation.	E. The social cognitive theory arose in response to behaviorism, which emphasizes the primacy of behavior over thought in learning.
C. Teachers use bright colors and odd shapes in their lessons to promote attentiveness on the part of their students.	F. Disinhibition is the encouragement and adoption of behaviors that are not considered socially acceptable.

LISTENING SECTION

Directions: In this section of the test, you will hear dialogues and academic talks, and you will be tested on your ability to understand them. You will hear each dialogue and academic talk only once, and then answer some questions after each is finished. The questions ask about the main idea, supporting details, and the way the speakers use language. Answer each question based on what is stated or implied by the speakers. You will be given 25–30 seconds to answer each question. You cannot go back to a question once you have answered it. Answer every question in the order that it appears.

While you listen, you may take notes. You can then use your notes when answering questions.

You will see the following headphones icon next to some questions: 🎧 This icon indicates that you will hear part of the dialogue or academic talk repeated for the question.

You will be given 20 minutes to answer all the questions in this section. This does not include the time to listen to the dialogues and academic talks.

Dialogue 1

 Track 1

Directions: Now use your notes to help you answer the questions.

1 Why does the student meet with the professor?

  (A) to join him for lunch

  (B) to ask for help with her homework

  (C) to inquire about earning extra credit

  (D) to discuss her grade on the 401 midterm

2 Does the professor normally accept extra credit projects?

  (A) Yes, he understands that students sometimes blank under pressure.

  (B) He sometimes does, but only if he develops the project ahead of time.

  (C) He usually does if the project is related to the coursework.

  (D) He usually doesn't, but may be open to a project that demonstrates the concept in depth.

3 Listen to part of the dialogue again, and then answer the question. Why does the professor say this?

  (A) to encourage the student to explain what happened during the test

  (B) to inquire where the student was during the midterm

  (C) to indicate that he thought the test was difficult

  (D) to demonstrate that he remembered the student's grade

4   What will the student do for extra credit?

    Ⓐ retake the exam

    Ⓑ retake the part of the exam she did poorly on

    Ⓒ write an explanation of why she did poorly on the test

    Ⓓ research concepts not covered in the book

5   What will the student probably do that afternoon?

    Ⓐ She will meet the professor in his office to discuss the project.

    Ⓑ She will work on her proposal for an extra credit assignment.

    Ⓒ She will study for the part of the exam she will retake.

    Ⓓ She will hand in a revision of her term paper.

Dialogue 2

Track 2

Directions: Now use your notes to help you answer the questions.

6   What is the professor referring to when he says WS?

    Ⓐ the Women's Shelter

    Ⓑ a Women's Seminar

    Ⓒ Women's Studies

    Ⓓ Women's Sociology

7   What else is required in addition to the coursework?

    Ⓐ completing an internship

    Ⓑ writing a term paper

    Ⓒ starting a community organization

    Ⓓ joining the National Organization for Women

8   What can be inferred about cross-disciplinary courses?

    Ⓐ Students can take the same course many times in different departments.

    Ⓑ Students can have the same professor for all their courses.

    Ⓒ Students are permitted to skip some courses and still complete their major.

    Ⓓ Students can take courses from different fields to complete their major.

9   Listen to part of the dialogue again, and then answer the question. What does the student's answer mean?

   Ⓐ She remembers the details of the requirements.

   Ⓑ She read the information too long ago to remember it.

   Ⓒ She already registered for all the courses she needs.

   Ⓓ She discussed the requirements with the professor months ago.

10 Why is the student looking forward to joining a women's organization?

   Ⓐ She wants to start her own organization.

   Ⓑ She hopes to bring some of her classmates to participate.

   Ⓒ She hopes to find a job by working there.

   Ⓓ She needs the money that she will receive from the organization.

Academic Talk 1: Art History

Track 3

Directions: Now use your notes to help you answer the questions.

11 What is the professor mainly discussing?

   Ⓐ the difference between public art and art in museums

   Ⓑ what famous critics have said about public art

   Ⓒ the characteristics of a work of public art

   Ⓓ graffiti in the New York City subway system

12 Listen to part of the talk again, and then answer the question. Why does the professor say this:

   Ⓐ to encourage the student to expand on his answer

   Ⓑ to express uncertainty about the facts

   Ⓒ to emphasize how important museums are to the public

   Ⓓ to criticize the student's answer

13 What are two of the key elements that are shared by most works of public art?

   Choose 2 answers.

   Ⓐ They are found in large cities.

   Ⓑ They are found in public places.

   Ⓒ They are controversial.

   Ⓓ They are on display for a short period of time.

14 Listen to part of the talk again, and then answer the question. What does the professor mean when she says this: 🎧

    Ⓐ The artists were unable to complete the project.

    Ⓑ The artists were unable to relocate the project.

    Ⓒ The project was on hold.

    Ⓓ The project dates had to be changed.

15 Listen to part of the talk again, and then answer the question.

How does the professor emphasize the fact that public art is considered controversial?

    Ⓐ by asking a series of questions

    Ⓑ by repeating the word *controversial*

    Ⓒ by citing how much money was spent on The Gates

    Ⓓ by reading the opinion of a well-known critic

16 Listen to part of the talk again, and then answer the question. What can be said about the professor?

    Ⓐ She assumes that the class has done the reading.

    Ⓑ She does not remember what the homework topic was.

    Ⓒ She expects to spend class time discussing the reading.

    Ⓓ She will not be asking about the topic again.

Academic Talk 2: Archaeology

🎧 **Track 4**

Directions: Now use your notes to help you answer the questions.

17 What is the talk mainly about?

    Ⓐ Animal mummies in ancient Egypt

    Ⓑ Egyptian beliefs about the afterlife

    Ⓒ The treatment of organs in mummification

    Ⓓ The process of making mummies

18 According to the talk, what did the Egyptians consider the most important organ?

    Ⓐ the brain

    Ⓑ the spleen

    Ⓒ the heart

    Ⓓ the lungs

19 According to the talk, which of the following can be inferred about Egyptian society?

    Ⓐ All Egyptians mummified their animals.

    Ⓑ Rich and poor were given the same advantages.

    Ⓒ A definite class structure was in place.

    Ⓓ Egyptians worshipped rich people.

20 Listen to part of the talk again, and then answer the question. Why does the professor say this: 🎧

    Ⓐ to show how little some people think about their brains

    Ⓑ to emphasize the importance of the brain

    Ⓒ to make a connection between movies and real life

    Ⓓ to introduce a famous experiment involving the brain

21 Listen to part of the talk again, and then answer the question. Why does the professor say this: 🎧

    Ⓐ He thinks some students will think this information is unpleasant.

    Ⓑ He knows this is a large amount of information to cover in one day.

    Ⓒ He wants the students to ask questions about embalming.

    Ⓓ He believes some of the students will find the information funny.

22 In the lecture, the professor describes the steps for mummification. Indicate whether each of the following is a step in this process.

	Yes	No
A. Removing the brain		
B. Wrapping all organs together		
C. Sealing cuts with cloth		
D. Massaging the body with oils		
E. Bandaging the body with linen		

Academic Talk 3: History

🎧 **Track 5**

Directions: Now use your notes to help you answer the questions.

23 What is the main topic of the lecture?

    Ⓐ The economic climate of the United States in the 1930s.

    Ⓑ The fame of bank robbers during the Great Depression.

    Ⓒ The origins of the Federal Bureau of Investigation.

    Ⓓ The first bank robberies in the United States.

24 According to the lecture, what did many Americans blame for the economic problems of the 1930s?

    Ⓐ bank robberies

    Ⓑ bank failures

    Ⓒ government agencies

    Ⓓ the 1929 stock market crash

25 According to the talk, why did J. Edgar Hoover want to capture John Dillinger?

    Ⓐ He wanted the public's admiration for himself.

    Ⓑ He thought Dillinger did not respect him.

    Ⓒ He wished to return the stolen money to the banks.

    Ⓓ He wanted to establish credibility for the FBI.

26 Why does the professor refer to the previous day's lecture?

    Ⓐ to emphasize that the Great Depression started in 1929

    Ⓑ to explain the causes of the Great Depression

    Ⓒ to relate the current topic to the previous topic

    Ⓓ to contrast it with the topic she is about to discuss

27 Listen to part of the talk again, and answer the question. What does the professor suggest?

    Ⓐ The public admired Dillinger even more as his crimes progressed.

    Ⓑ Dillinger's crimes were very famous.

    Ⓒ Dillinger did not kill often, so he wasn't very dangerous.

    Ⓓ The public was not very concerned with Dillinger after a while.

28 According to the discussion, which of the following statements could describe the general feeling of the American public in the 1930s?

Choose 3 answers.

- A They were frustrated by the continuing financial crisis.
- B They blamed financial institutions for causing the Great Depression.
- C They were more afraid of the police than the Dillinger Gang.
- D They were cautious in supporting the FBI.
- E They were angered by the banks' insensitivity to poor people.

Academic Talk 4: Literature

Track 6

Directions: Now use your notes to help you answer the questions.

29 What is the lecture mainly about?

- A the works of Edgar Allan Poe
- B effective literary devices
- C the importance of reading a work more than once
- D common types of symbolism

30 Why does the professor talk about symbolism?

- A to introduce the concept of implied meaning
- B to compare it to point of view
- C to explain the qualities of a good poem
- D to give an example of a literary device that is often misunderstood

31 According to the professor, how do symbolism and foreshadowing differ?

- A Symbolism is easier to see than foreshadowing.
- B Symbolism is harder to use than foreshadowing.
- C Symbolism is less effective than foreshadowing.
- D Symbolism makes a work more difficult to read than foreshadowing.

32 Listen to part of the talk again, and then answer the question. What does the professor imply?

  (A) It is not always necessary for the reader to understand everything to enjoy a work of literature.

  (B) By reading widely it is possible to become more skilled at finding hidden references in literature.

  (C) It is much better for an author not to reveal too much to the reader in the early stages of a work.

  (D) Works often require more than one reading for full understanding.

33 What does the professor say about the work *A Jury of Her Peers*?

  (A) It uses foreshadowing more extensively than a play does.

  (B) It demonstrates that authors can create several different effects from one idea.

  (C) The title makes the author's use of foreshadowing more explicit.

  (D) The students should become familiar with the work.

34 Listen to part of the talk again, and then answer the question. What can be inferred from the professor's statement?

  (A) Poe used foreshadowing better than his contemporaries did.

  (B) Many authors use foreshadowing successfully.

  (C) Poe created the device known as foreshadowing.

  (D) Other authors have learned from Poe's example.

SPEAKING SECTION

Directions: In this section, you will be asked to respond to a variety of tasks and topics. There are six tasks. Respond to each task as completely as you can, always speaking clearly.

For tasks 1 and 2, you will speak about topics that are familiar to you. Your responses will be graded on your ability to speak about the topics clearly.

For tasks 3 and 4, you will be asked to read a short text. The text will then go off the screen and you will hear a talk on the same topic. For each task, you will be asked a question about what you have read and heard. You will need to use information from the text and the talk to answer the questions. Your responses will be graded on your ability to speak clearly and accurately about what you have read and heard.

For tasks 5 and 6, you will hear part of a dialogue or an academic talk. For each task, you will then answer a question about what you have heard. Your responses will be graded on your ability to speak clearly and accurately about what you have heard.

You are allowed to take notes during the reading and listening. You are allowed to use your notes to help you respond. Listen closely to the directions for each task.

For each task, you will be given a short time to prepare your response. You will be given a certain amount of time to speak. Use a watch or clock to time yourself.

Task 1

Directions: For this task, you will be asked to speak about a topic that is familiar to you. You will hear a question. You will then have 15 seconds to prepare your response and 45 seconds to speak.

 Track 7

Describe the best gift you ever received and say what made the gift so special. Give details to support your choice.

> 15 seconds to prepare
> 45 seconds to speak

Task 2

Directions: For this task, you will give your opinion about a topic that is familiar to you. You will hear a question. You will then have 15 seconds to prepare your response and 45 seconds to speak.

 Track 8

Some students prefer to study alone. Others prefer to study with a friend, or in a group. Which method do you prefer and why? Give details and examples in your explanation.

> 15 seconds to prepare
> 45 seconds to speak

Task 3

Directions: For this task, you will read a short text and then listen to a dialogue about the same topic. You will hear a question about what you have read and heard. You will then have 30 seconds to prepare your response and 60 seconds to speak.

City University has hired a new president. Read the announcement from the board of trustees. You have 45 seconds to read the passage. Begin reading now.

An Announcement from the Board of Trustees

The Board of Trustees is pleased to announce that the university has selected Victor C. Mullins to be the university's 25th president. Mullins will succeed Dr. James White, who announced his retirement in July.

Victor Mullins comes to City University after having served 16 years in the United States Senate. Prior to becoming a senator, he worked in his family's real estate business.

In a statement released yesterday, the Board of Trustees cited Mullins's "extensive administrative and financial experience" as the primary reason for selecting him to head the institution.

 Track 9

The woman expresses her opinion of a recent decision made by the university. State her opinion and explain the reasons she gives for holding that opinion.

> 30 seconds to prepare
> 60 seconds to speak

Task 4

Directions: For this task, you will read a short text and then hear a talk about the same topic. You will hear a question about what you have read and heard. After you hear the question, you will have 30 seconds to prepare your response and 60 seconds to speak.

Now read the passage about the Bretton Woods conference. You have 45 seconds to read the passage. Begin reading now.

A Meeting at Bretton Woods

In July 1944, the leaders of 44 nations gathered in a small New England town to set the rules for monetary relations between the major industrialized powers. The most influential countries at Bretton Woods, led by the United States, were united in the belief that a strong international economic system would lead to economic security, which would, in turn, help ensure peace.

As part of their effort to achieve economic stability, the nations gathered at Bretton Woods agreed to maintain fixed exchange rates for their currencies, anchored by the United States' guarantee to redeem international dollar holdings at the rate of $35 per ounce of gold. The Bretton Woods system remained in place relatively unchanged until the early 1970s.

Track 10

The professor talked about the end of the Bretton Woods system. Explain what the purpose of the Bretton Woods system was and how and why it ended. Give details and examples to support your answer.

> 30 seconds to prepare
> 60 seconds to speak

Task 5

Directions: For this task, you will listen to a dialogue. You will hear a question about it. You will then have 20 seconds to prepare your response and 60 seconds to speak.

 Track 11

The students discuss possible solutions to the man's problem. Describe the problem. Then state which of the solutions you prefer and explain why.

> 20 seconds to prepare
> 60 seconds to speak

Task 6

Directions: For this task, you will hear a short academic talk. You will hear a question about it. You will then have 20 seconds to prepare your response and 60 seconds to speak.

 Track 12

Using points and examples from the talk, explain how a price war between two competing retail stores reflects the principles of game theory.

> 20 seconds to prepare
> 60 seconds to speak

WRITING SECTION

Directions: You will need your headphones for this section.

This section is designed to measure your ability to write in English. There are two tasks.

For the first task, you will read a short text and listen to an academic talk. You will answer a question about what you have read and heard. For the second task, you will use your knowledge and experience to answer a question.

Task 1

Directions: For this task, you will have 3 minutes to read a short text. You may take notes if you wish. Then you will hear an academic talk on the same topic. You may take notes while you listen.

You will then read a question that asks about the relationship between the text and the talk. You will have 20 minutes to write a response. Using information from the text and talk, answer the question as completely as you can. You will **not** be asked to give your opinion. You will be able to review the text while you write. You may use your notes to help you write your response.

You should try to write 150 words or more. Your response will be graded on the quality, completeness, and accuracy of your writing. If you finish early, you may move on to the second task.

In this question, you will read a short passage and then listen to a lecture on the same topic. You will then have 20 minutes to write an answer to the question that follows, using your notes and the written passage for reference.

You now have 3 minutes to read the passage. After you read the passage, listen to the talk.

"Global warming" is defined as an increase in the earth's atmospheric temperature. Causes of global warming can be categorized in two ways: human-induced warming and natural climate fluctuations that have been in place for thousands of years.

Many scientists believe that human activity has very little, if any, impact on the recent warming trend on Earth. These researchers point to the various ice ages in the earth's history, the most recent of which occurred 15,000 years ago, almost 14,000 years before industry and human habitation had any impact on the atmosphere. While not as well documented, these ice ages might have been tempered by warmer periods throughout history—meaning the current increase in the earth's atmospheric temperature is nothing more than a cyclical natural phenomenon.

In fact, it is difficult to determine the impact of humans on the environment as we have only been documenting weather changes for the last 100 years. Most scientists agree that data from a longer time period is needed to build an accurate picture of temperature fluctuations. Over the past 100 years, the temperature has only risen marginally—about one degree. This warming has not been uniform, as some areas of the world have actually experienced cooling over the past 20 years, even with record activity caused by El Niño in 1997 and 1998.

In reality, there is no conclusive evidence that human activity has any effect on the earth's surface temperature. While environmental activists and other alarmists are quick to blame increased carbon dioxide emissions for the recent trend, the truth is that nobody knows whether a similar warming—and cyclical cooling—occurred before the advent of temperature-related technology in the late 1900s.

 ## Track 13

Summarize the points made in the lecture you just heard, explaining how they cast doubt on points made in the reading.

Task 2

For this task, you will be asked to write an essay in which you state, explain, and support your opinion on an issue. You will have 30 minutes to complete your essay.

You should try to write 300 words or more. Your essay will be graded on how well you use language, organize your essay, and develop your ideas.

Do you agree or disagree with the following statement?

Children should be occupied at all times and should never be left unsupervised.

Use specific reasons to support your answer.

Practice Test 2

TEST DIRECTIONS

This test is designed to measure your ability to understand and to use English in an academic context. The test has four sections.

In the **Reading** section, you will read three passages and answer questions about them.

In the **Listening** section, you will listen to two dialogues and four talks and answer questions about them.

In the **Speaking** section, there are six tasks. The first two tasks ask you to speak based on your own personal experience. In the other four, you will read passages and/or listen to dialogues and talks, then speak based on what you have read and/or heard.

In the **Writing** section, there are two tasks. In the first task, you will read a passage, listen to a talk, then write based on what you have read and heard. The second task asks you to write based on your own personal experience and ideas.

There is a 10-minute break after the **Listening** section.

At the beginning of each section, there are directions that explain how to answer the questions or respond to the tasks in the section.

In the **Reading** and **Listening** sections, you should work carefully but quickly. You should try to answer every question to the best of your ability. Make an educated guess on questions that you are unsure of. In the **Speaking** and **Writing** sections, each task is separately timed. In each case, you should try to respond to the task as completely as possible in the given time.

READING SECTION

Directions: In this section of the test, you will read three passages. You will be tested on your ability to understand them by answering several questions on each passage.

While you read, you may take notes. You can then use your notes when answering questions.

Most questions are worth one point. Questions that are worth more than one point have a special note telling you how many total points they are worth.

You will have 60 minutes to read the three passages and answer all the questions. If you finish the questions before 60 minutes is up, you can go back and review your work in this section.

Passage 1

How Satellites Have Revolutionized Communication

A satellite is any object that orbits a celestial body. The moon is considered to be the earth's largest natural satellite. Artificial satellites at one time were perceived as top-secret devices used by spies, military agents, and science fiction characters. But today, there are many practical uses for modern satellites, including weather forecasting, television transmission, global positioning systems (GPS), astronomy, and accurate mapping of the earth.

Prior to the advent of satellites, electronic communication was primarily accomplished via wires and cables strung between high towers and run underground. Science fiction writer Arthur C. Clarke was the first to envision using man-made satellites as communication devices. In an article released in a 1945 edition of *Wireless World* magazine, he described a worldwide coverage network using three satellites placed 120 degrees apart in Earth's orbit. Of course, Clarke's vision wasn't entirely science fiction. Today's technology allows communication to occur regularly between all parts of the world via wireless satellite transmissions.

Most satellites fall into one of two orbital categories, GEO or non-GEO. Satellites in a GEO (Geostationary Earth Orbit) maintain 24-hour synchronization with the earth's orbit and appear in a fixed spot above the earth at all times. These satellites orbit higher than 22,000 miles (36,000 km), cover entire hemispheres at once, and are generally used for weather forecasting and communications. Non-GEO satellites generally travel lower than the GEO satellites and have an asynchronous orbit, meaning they move independently of the Earth's orbit. As a result, at various times they can be seen passing overhead as they move across the sky. Non-GEO satellites have a shorter range and footprint area and are generally used for observation, photography, scientific studies, and navigation.

On October 4, 1957, under extreme secrecy, the Soviets launched the *Sputnik 1* satellite into orbit. It was a very simple, 184-pound ball that only lasted 92 days before burning up in the earth's atmosphere. The apparent superiority of the Soviet space program both embarrassed and frightened U.S. citizens. The event fueled America's race to space, which led to the historical U.S. moon landing and the subsequent creation of the International Space Station.

Satellites are used for various aspects of everyday life, from live cable news coverage to military intelligence monitoring. The military uses satellites to track enemy movement, monitor nuclear activity, provide early warnings of missile launching, and photograph inaccessible areas of foreign lands. Scientists have been able to use satellite technology to study global warming, monitor plants and animals, and—by putting observational satellites in orbit, like the Hubble Space Telescope—open windows to the universe. A network of Global Positioning System (GPS) satellites is used to determine exact locations of cars, planes, trains, ships, and humans. Right now, there isn't very much of the earth's soil that isn't monitored by thousands of orbiting satellites.

Satellite technology has made the world a much smaller and, arguably, a safer place to live. Through satellite tracking, meteorologists can provide early warnings about large storms or tornados, which saves hundreds of lives every year. **A** Knowing when and where a missile may be launched helps the military warn civilians of impending danger and enables soldiers to destroy the missile before it reaches its intended target. **B** What once took days or weeks of travel—for example, a face-to-face conversation with a long-distance relative—can now be achieved in seconds with satellite communication technology. **C**

Satellites are even sent as probes to distant planets so we can explore our solar system and its complexity. **D** The galaxy is extremely large, and due to the current limitations of space travel technology, it is impossible to send manned missions to distant locations. Satellites act as human eyes and ears, monitoring distant planets for signs of life outside of Earth. If humans ever do find new life-forms in space, it is likely that satellites will establish our first contact. Unfortunately, this is still science fiction.

1   According to the passage, Arthur C. Clarke played an important role in the development of artificial satellites because

   (A) he conceived of a global system of satellites used for communication.
   (B) he imagined the possibility of sending a satellite into orbit around the earth.
   (C) he published *Wireless World*, which elevated satellites above science fiction.
   (D) he was the first person to envision the development of artificial satellites.

2   The word envision in the passage is closest in meaning to

   (A) see.
   (B) imagine.
   (C) engineer.
   (D) propose.

3   The word fueled in the passage is closest in meaning to

   (A) propelled.
   (B) fed.
   (C) complicated.
   (D) humiliated.

4 According to the information in paragraph 3, GEO satellites differ from non-GEO satellites in all of the following ways EXCEPT

(A) GEO satellites are further from the earth.

(B) GEO satellites are more commonly used for scientific studies.

(C) GEO satellites move along with the Earth's orbit and appear stationary.

(D) GEO satellites cover a larger geographic area of the earth.

5 The author discusses the Soviet space program in paragraph 4 in order to

(A) show how it spurred innovation in the United States' own space program.

(B) compare Soviet science education with the United States'.

(C) justify the premise that a satellite technology need not be very sophisticated.

(D) provide an example of a satellite that could only stay aloft for a short time.

6 From the information in paragraph 5, it can be inferred that

(A) most of the world can be surveyed by satellites.

(B) the primary use of most satellites is for military purposes.

(C) satellites have been used to prove that global warming is man-made.

(D) GPS technology is growing in popularity.

7 Look at the four letters (**A**, **B**, **C**, and **D**) in the passage that show where the following sentence could be inserted.

Moreover, satellites have enabled developing countries to make use of modern communication technologies without having to construct costly wire and cable infrastructures.

Where would the sentence best fit in the passage? Choose the letter for the square where this sentence should be added.

8 The word impending in the passage is closest in meaning to

(A) horrible.

(B) military.

(C) awaiting.

(D) coming.

9   Which of the following sentences most closely expresses the important information in the highlighted sentence in the passage?

     (A) For now, the galaxy's size and the inadequacy of technology prevents manned missions to remote parts of the galaxy.

     (B) Because of the galaxy's size and mankind's present technological shortcomings, sending a satellite far into the galaxy is not possible.

     (C) Since the galaxy is huge and our technology limited, it will be a while before we will be able to travel to faraway locations in the cosmos.

     (D) The great size of the galaxy makes sending a human to distant parts of the universe technically very difficult.

10   Which of the following statements most accurately reflects the author's opinion about artificial satellites?

     (A) While satellites have served many useful purposes, their proliferation may pose problems in the future.

     (B) What is most valuable about satellites is their potential to discover other life-forms in the universe.

     (C) Satellites have greatly increased our knowledge of the world and our ability to communicate with each other.

     (D) Without satellites, long-distance communication and meteorological forecasting would be impossible.

11   According to the passage, satellites are useful in the transmission of information mainly because

     (A) they do not rely on wires and cables strung between high towers.

     (B) they can receive and send data over large areas of the earth.

     (C) they can transmit information in an inefficient but affordable manner.

     (D) they can transmit data from earth to distant parts of the universe.

12 Directions: Below is an introductory sentence for a short summary of the passage. Complete the summary by choosing the THREE answer choices that express key ideas in the passage. Sentences that express ideas that are NOT in the passage or mention minor details do NOT belong in the summary. *This question is worth 2 points.*

Satellites have revolutionized our ability to communicate with each other and observe our world, as well as worlds beyond.

Answer Choices	
A. Before the development of artificial satellites, the idea of long-distance communication without wires was only the stuff of science fiction.	D. Among the most important uses for satellites today are mass communications, meteorological forecasting, and scientific study.
B. Arthur C. Clarke envisioned satellites long before we were technologically capable of sending them into space.	E. Scientists are confident that one day soon a satellite will discover other intelligent life-forms in outer space.
C. There are two kinds of satellites: GEO, which follow the earth's orbit, and non-GEO, which move independently of the earth's orbit.	F. In 1957, the Soviets launched *Sputnik*, a 184-pound ball that spent three months in space before burning up in the earth's atmosphere.

Passage 2

Alexander Hamilton: America's Visionary Economist

History books are full of accounts of how Alexander Hamilton was a visionary* who made political and military contributions toward the establishment of a strong federal government for the United States. Overcoming the formidable political opposition of Thomas Jefferson, James Madison, and John Adams—all of whom would become president—Hamilton not only devised a successful system of credit and mercantilism but also helped design and organize the national banking system.

Hamilton was both creative and practical. After the revolution against England, all 13 states and the federal government fell into debt. As Hamilton noticed that the banking system of England was efficient and successful, he used this banking model and designed a banking system which allowed the federal government to assume the debt of the states in the interest of gaining positive standing in the international trading world of the 18th century.

As the secretary of the treasury under President George Washington, Hamilton devised a system of taxation that would both pay down the national debt and bring the federal government and the 13 states into a closer and more cooperative relationship. His financial acumen and creative problem-solving ability would be recognized today as true "nation building." Although his vision did not reach as far forward as the 21st century, he did lay the groundwork for a system of trade.

That system took into account the reality of his time. France, England, and Spain still controlled vast territories in North America and remained powers to be reckoned with. Hamilton's desire was to make the United States a truly independent nation both ideologically and economically. Although he agreed that the country was a great farming nation and its agrarian potential should be exploited, he foresaw that only with the addition of industrialization would America achieve true and total independence.

On December 5, 1791, Hamilton, in his role as secretary of the treasury, delivered a report to the House of Representatives titled, "Report on Manufactures." In this report, Hamilton set forth his vision for economic independence. The country, Hamilton told the representatives, must do two things. First, it must find a way to profitably increase demand for produce at home. Second, a system of manufacturing must be devised to reduce the need for goods supplied from abroad. The achievement of these two goals, stated Hamilton, "[would be] favorable to national independence and safety."

He also made the point that the agricultural success could and must be the foundation for expanding America's business into the area of "manufactures." The secretary's speech was carefully structured to acknowledge the country's success to date and at the same time open the representatives' minds to the idea of manufacturing as a national focus. He did not argue for manufacturing at the expense of agriculture, but rather for a "cogent and persuasive national policy" that would enhance both the maximization of land use and the establishment of an added focus on manufacturing. His claim, again, was that this dual endeavor would make the United States more independent and powerful.

Hamilton proceeded to share his vision of a country that included both successful farmers and manufacturers, each elevating the status of the other. "Each furnishes a certain portion of the produce of his labor to the other," he told the representatives. After outlining his proposal, Hamilton provided the audience with a list of clear and simple consequences that would flow from his plan.

Hamilton meant to secure the borders, foster efficient prosperity, and put the United States on equal footing with its trading partners around the globe. His report goes into minute detail regarding the impact of these circumstances on the nation. Now, in the 21st century, one can look back and see Alexander Hamilton not as just one of the founding fathers of a republican experiment but as a true economic visionary.

A Unfortunately, Hamilton did not live long enough to appreciate the outcome of his economic vision. **B** His power and skill in the arena of policy and debate did not serve him as well in the field of real combat. **C** He died in 1804 in a duel with his personal and political rival Aaron Burr, then vice president to Thomas Jefferson. **D** His face is immortalized on the ten-dollar bill.

Visionary: a person with intelligent ideas about how things should be in the future.

13 It can be inferred from the passage that all of the following were U.S. presidents EXCEPT

- (A) Thomas Jefferson.
- (B) James Madison.
- (C) Alexander Hamilton.
- (D) John Adams.

14 The word devised in the passage is closest in meaning to

- (A) produced.
- (B) created.
- (C) determined.
- (D) funded.

15 According to the passage, Hamilton deserves credit for all of the following EXCEPT

- (A) reducing the national debt through the creation of a system of taxation.
- (B) fostering economic cooperation between states and the federal government.
- (C) promoting industrialization without undermining the agricultural system.
- (D) developing and implementing an original banking model for the United States.

16 The word acumen in the passage is closest in meaning to

- (A) partners.
- (B) education.
- (C) wealth.
- (D) insight.

17 Who was the audience for Hamilton's "Report on Manufactures"?

- (A) the president and his cabinet
- (B) businessmen and farmers
- (C) the House of Representatives
- (D) the Senate

18 According to the passage, the recommendations in Hamilton's "Report on Manufactures" were mainly motivated by a desire

- (A) to make the United States more independent.
- (B) to build stronger alliances with world trading powers.
- (C) to win political support for President Washington.
- (D) to promote the interests of the nation's industrialists.

19 The quotes from Hamilton's "Report on Manufactures" in paragraph 7 are meant to

(A) emphasize the mutual benefits of increasing manufacturing for both farmers and manufacturers.

(B) argue for increasing manufacturing, despite the adverse consequences for farmers.

(C) demonstrate Hamilton's eloquence in making an argument before a large group.

(D) reflect Hamilton's belief in a dual system of commerce that would rely on farmers.

20 Look at the four letters (**A**, **B**, **C**, and **D**) in the passage that show where the following sentence could be inserted.

Hamilton's contributions to the country, however, have not gone unrecognized.

Where would the sentence best fit in the passage? Choose the letter for the square where this sentence should be added.

21 It can be inferred from the passage that the United States attained the status of a world economic superpower

(A) in the 18th century.

(B) after Hamilton died.

(C) shortly after the Revolutionary War.

(D) late in Hamilton's life.

22 According to the passage, the main reason Alexander Hamilton is an important figure in American history is

(A) he helped transform the nation into a future world economic power

(B) he delivered the highly influential "Report on Manufactures".

(C) he was the first to advocate a shift from agriculture to manufacturing.

(D) he fought against creating a strong federal banking system.

23 **Directions:** Below is an introductory sentence for a short summary of the passage. Complete the summary by choosing the THREE answer choices that express key ideas in the passage. Sentences that express ideas that are NOT in the passage or mention minor details do NOT belong in the summary. *This question is worth 2 points.*

Many historians regard Alexander Hamilton as the economic founding father of America.

Answer Choices	
A. Hamilton went to great lengths to assure farmers that his plan in no way supported manufacturing at their expense.	D. Hamilton's face today adorns the ten-dollar bill.
B. Hamilton reformed the U.S. banking and tax system to help the country emerge from debt.	E. The policies outlined in the report are credited with setting the nation on the course it would take toward world economic dominance.
C. In his famous "Report on Manufactures," Hamilton promoted a greater economic emphasis on manufacturing.	F. Hamilton was known for his great self-confidence, which sometimes came across as arrogance and led to a fatal duel.

Passage 3

The Incandescent Lightbulb

The active component of a "normal" lightbulb, properly referred to as an incandescent bulb, consists of a thin wire made of a hard metallic element, tungsten, housed inside a glass container. The tungsten wire is called the filament.

The basic idea behind these bulbs is simple. When the bulb is used, electricity flows through the filament, which is so thin that it offers considerable resistance to the flow of electricity, and this resistance turns electrical energy into heat. The heat produced is enough to make the filament emit light. The emission of visible light by any hot object is called incandescence. Some examples of incandescent objects are hot coals in a campfire or barbecue grill, the sun, and a red, glowing burner on an electric stove when the temperature is high. The higher the temperature of the incandescent object, the brighter the light that is given off.

To optimize the visible light emitted and the longevity of a filament, the material used for the filament must withstand high temperatures without melting or reacting. Many filament materials were evaluated in the attempt to create optimum visible-light emission and filament longevity. Early lightbulbs used filaments of carbon. However, a carbon filament will not last long at temperatures higher than 2,100°C before it vaporizes. At lower filament temperatures, a carbon-filament bulb gives off only dim light. The tungsten filament used in today's lightbulb does not melt because tungsten has a very high melting point (6,100°F, or 3,370°C). Because most of the air has been sucked out of a glass lightbulb, there is no oxygen to react with, or oxidize, the filament. Consequently, tungsten filaments last a comparatively long time.

Although tungsten filaments offer the best combination of high melting point and low vapor pressure of any known elemental filament material, they eventually fail because of evaporation. The heat causes the tungsten to slowly evaporate, thus narrowing the diameter of the filament. This increases the electrical resistance (due to the smaller cross-section of the wire), and causes the filament to heat up more, which in turn increases the evaporation rate even further. Eventually, the filament fails. The black on the inside of a burned-out lightbulb is tungsten vapor returned to solid form. Besides their limited life spans, incandescent lightbulbs also waste a lot of electricity. Heat is not light, so all of the energy consumed by resistance is wasted.

A fluorescent bulb, however, uses a completely different method to produce light. This bulb consists of a glass tube with an electrode at each end. Inside the tube is a gas containing argon and mercury vapor. As electricity flows through the tube, a stream of electrons flows through the gas from one electrode to the other. These electrons collide with the mercury atoms and raise them to a higher-energy, or "excited," state. As the mercury atoms move from the excited state back to the unexcited state, they emit this acquired energy in the form of packets of light—photons—in the ultraviolet region of the spectrum. These ultraviolet photons hit a phosphor coating on the inside of the tube and cause this phosphor to emit visible light, to 'fluoresce,' in other words. Since in a fluorescent bulb the emission of light is caused by electricity and not by heat, the bulb can be much cooler than an incandescent bulb. Since a fluorescent bulb is cooler, there is nothing to vaporize, and therefore the bulb lasts longer.

Since fluorescent bulbs produce less heat than incandescent bulbs do, they are much more efficient. **A** A fluorescent bulb produces between four and six times as much light per watt as an incandescent bulb does. **B** This is why a 15-watt fluorescent bulb and a 60-watt incandescent bulb produce the same amount of light. **C** Still, as efficient and economical as they may be, fluorescent bulbs have not supplanted incandescent ones. **D**

24 The word emit in the passage is closest in meaning to

   Ⓐ cause.

   Ⓑ give off.

   Ⓒ circulate.

   Ⓓ reflect.

25 Which of the following is most likely NOT an example of incandescence?

   Ⓐ reflected light

   Ⓑ a car cigarette lighter

   Ⓒ a star

   Ⓓ molten iron

26 Based on information in paragraph 2, which of the following best describes the term incandescence?

   Ⓐ The light released by burning of heat-resistant material.

   Ⓑ The release of light as a consequence of heat.

   Ⓒ The heat produced by electricity as it flows through resistance.

   Ⓓ The generation of heat due to an increase in light intensity.

27 Which of the following sentences most closely expresses the important information in the highlighted sentence in the passage?

   Ⓐ The heat of the object is influenced by its brightness.

   Ⓑ The object's brightness rises in proportion to its temperature.

   Ⓒ The heat of the incandescent object corresponds to its dimness.

   Ⓓ Raising the temperature of the object creates a warmer light.

28 The word withstand in the passage is closest in meaning to

   Ⓐ produce.

   Ⓑ uphold.

   Ⓒ endure.

   Ⓓ maintain.

29 According to the passage, the main reason tungsten filaments were deemed superior to carbon ones was

   Ⓐ tungsten never burns out.

   Ⓑ carbon gives off a dimmer light.

   Ⓒ tungsten is more resistant to heat.

   Ⓓ carbon requires more energy to illuminate.

30 According to the passage, fluorescent bulbs last longer than incandescent ones because

   Ⓐ they can withstand much higher temperatures.

   Ⓑ they are more durable.

   Ⓒ they do not produce vaporizing heat.

   Ⓓ their electrodes prevent vaporization.

31 Fluorescent bulbs are described in paragraph 5 in order to

   Ⓐ contrast them to less efficient tungsten bulbs.

   Ⓑ show how they are less efficient than incandescent bulbs.

   Ⓒ provide an example of a more sophisticated incandescent bulb.

   Ⓓ conclude that they are superior to incandescent bulbs.

32 Look at the four letters (**A**, **B**, **C**, and **D**) in the passage that show where the following sentence could be inserted.

Whether for sentimental or aesthetic reasons, tungsten-filament bulbs remain popular.

Where would the sentence best fit in the passage? Choose the letter for the square where this sentence should be added.

33 The word supplanted in the passage is closest in meaning to

(A) removed.

(B) outgrown.

(C) outsold.

(D) displaced.

34 It can be inferred that incandescent bulbs today

(A) are preferred by consumers.

(B) produce inferior quality light.

(C) cost more than fluorescent bulbs.

(D) are becoming increasingly uncommon.

35 According to the passage, what is the main difference between an incandescent bulb and a fluorescent bulb?

(A) An incandescent bulb is housed in a glass container.

(B) An incandescent bulb produces light more efficiently.

(C) A fluorescent bulb produces light from electricity, not heat.

(D) A fluorescent bulb produces light without generating heat.

36 **Directions:** Find the phrases in the answer choices list that relate to the type of bulb listed. Write your answers in the appropriate place. TWO of the answer choices will NOT match either category. *This question is worth 4 points.*

Answer Choices	Incandescent bulbs
A. Have filaments	
B. Produces ultraviolet light	
C. The formation of photons	
D. The conversion of heat energy to light	**Fluorescent bulbs**
E. The use of chemical reactions to generate light	
F. Similar to the glowing of red-hot metal	
G. The generation of light without electricity	
H. The use of electrodes	
I. Able to withstand very high temperatures	

LISTENING SECTION

Directions: In this section of the test, you will hear dialogues and academic talks, and you will be tested on your ability to understand them. You will hear each dialogue and academic talk only once, and then answer some questions after each is finished. The questions ask about the main idea, supporting details, and the way the speakers use language. Answer each question based on what is stated or implied by the speakers. You cannot go back to a question once you have answered it. Answer every question in the order that it appears.

While you listen, you may take notes. You can then use your notes when answering questions.

You will see the following headphones icon next to some questions: ∩ This icon indicates that you will hear part of the dialogue or academic talk repeated for the question.

Most questions are worth one point. Questions that are worth more than one point have a special note telling you how many total points they are worth.

You will be given 20 minutes to answer all the questions in this section. This does not include the time to listen to the dialogues and academic talks.

Dialogue 1

 Track 14

Directions: Now use your notes to help you answer the questions.

1   How did the student learn about the peer advisement program?

   (A) from a sign on the door
   (B) from a flyer on campus
   (C) from an open house
   (D) from an email

2   Why should the student attend the open house?

   (A) to meet her professors
   (B) to earn a credit toward her degree
   (C) to see where she would be working
   (D) to get more information about the program

3   What can be inferred about the peer advisor?

   (A) He is a transfer student.
   (B) He is a licensed counselor.
   (C) He is ready to leave the program.
   (D) He is enthusiastic about the program

4   Listen to part of the dialogue again, and then answer the question. What does the peer advisor mean when he says this:

    Ⓐ He wants to know if the student would like a snack.

    Ⓑ He wants to offer some counseling to the student.

    Ⓒ He plans to summarize the program for the student.

    Ⓓ He does not know much about the program himself.

5   Listen to part of the dialogue again, and then answer the question. What does the student mean when she says this: 🎧

    Ⓐ She wonders if she might have to deal with serious cases.

    Ⓑ She thinks the courses will be too intense for her.

    Ⓒ She wants to know if the counselors also have weekend duties.

    Ⓓ She hopes she will meet many experienced counselors.

Dialogue 2

🎧 **Track 15**

Directions: Now use your notes to help you answer the questions.

6   Why does the manager think the student looks familiar?

    Ⓐ She has seen him in a restaurant many times.

    Ⓑ She had worked with him in the past.

    Ⓒ He frequently visits the bookstore.

    Ⓓ He brought her his résumé a few days earlier.

7   What can be inferred about the manager?

    Ⓐ She thinks the student is overqualified for the job.

    Ⓑ She does not feel like making dinner after working all day.

    Ⓒ She is unhappy about having to work late.

    Ⓓ She has to work at the cash registers during the busy time.

8 Why does the student offer to go home and get his résumé?

(A) He is afraid someone else will get the job.

(B) He knows the manager is too busy to see him now.

(C) He forgot to bring it with him and is sorry.

(D) He thinks the manager will eat at the diner later.

9 Listen to part of the dialogue again, and then answer the question. What does the manager mean when she says this: 🎧

(A) The store will also be very busy.

(B) The store staff will be tired from all the work.

(C) The bookstore will be messy because of renovation work.

(D) The customers will not know where the books will be.

10 Listen to part of the dialogue again, and then answer the question. Why is the student surprised?

(A) He cannot understand why students waste money buying unnecessary books.

(B) He cannot understand why students return books right after starting class.

(C) He thinks the manager must be mistaken about the timing.

(D) He thinks the store should not accept returns until later in the semester.

Academic Talk 1: Music

🎧 **Track 16**

Directions: Now use your notes to help you answer the questions.

11 What is the talk mainly about?

(A) How recorded music eventually came to replace live performances.

(B) How recording techniques and music performance styles have changed.

(C) How Edison's original concept of the phonograph had to change.

(D) How classical music helped the phonograph industry to become profitable.

12 Why does the professor talk about Edison's attempts to market the phonograph as a dictation machine?

(A) to explain why it took a long time for music recording to get established

(B) to criticize Edison and show that even great inventors can make mistakes

(C) to illustrate the relationship of big business to the success of inventions demonstrate that without the support of business, the phonograph would never have developed

(D) to give an example of an invention that, over time, changed its function

13 Listen to part of the talk again, and then answer the question. What does the professor imply?

  Ⓐ It would be hard to hear classical music clearly in saloons and fairgrounds.

  Ⓑ The first recordings of Bach and Beethoven were surprisingly successful.

  Ⓒ Fairground and saloon owners wanted music of wide appeal.

  Ⓓ Fairground and saloon patrons had sophisticated musical taste.

14 What does the professor say about Caruso?

  Ⓐ He was one of the loudest singers ever.

  Ⓑ His performing style was introverted and refined.

  Ⓒ He began his career performing in fairgrounds and saloons.

  Ⓓ He helped to give the phonograph credibility.

15 What does the professor say about Edison and music?

  Ⓐ He enjoyed opera, coronet solos, and Caruso's performances.

  Ⓑ He was not very musical but did his best to learn more about it.

  Ⓒ He investigated the commercial potential of music systematically.

  Ⓓ He built up a very important archive of recordings of classical music.

16 According to the talk, which of the following are true of sound recording?

Choose 3 answers.

  A̲ It was quickly accepted by classical musicians.

  B̲ It has allowed musicians to become more self-critical.

  C̲ It led to the spread of international styles in performing.

  D̲ Studio and live performances are often very different.

  E̲ There was a huge demand for music recordings at first.

Academic Talk 2: Film History

 Track 17

Directions: Now use your notes to help you answer the questions.

17 What is the talk mainly about?

  Ⓐ The use of color in film.

  Ⓑ Film as truth and art.

  Ⓒ The impact of edited images.

  Ⓓ Acting methods in film.

18 What is the overall effect of combining images in a montage?

(A) Combining multiple images can create new meanings for the viewer.

(B) Using many images indicates the filmmaker's inability to tell a clear story.

(C) Combining multiple images makes the viewer suspend judgment about content.

(D) Combining many different images creates new color associations in the mind's eye.

19 Listen to part of the talk again, and then answer the question. What can be inferred from this comment by the professor: 🎧

(A) Chemicals in the film work together to merge the images.

(B) The images interact rapidly to create something new.

(C) It is helpful if filmmakers are familiar with the science of color.

(D) The images create a chemical reaction in the viewer's brain.

20 Listen to part of the talk again, and then answer the question. Why does the professor say this: 🎧

(A) to express uncertainty about the judgment of the viewers

(B) to prompt students to pay attention and answer the question

(C) to introduce the definition of dialectical filmmaking

(D) to suggest that what seems obvious is in fact the opposite

21 Listen to part of the talk again, and then answer the question. What does the professor mean when she says this: 🎧

(A) He believes that watching films too often can hurt one's eyes.

(B) He thinks that the brain functions as an eye, but sees colors differently.

(C) He thinks the brain and the eye work together to create a new impression.

(D) He means that the eye is not affected by contrasting colors.

22 Which of the following does the professor compare film to in the lecture?

Choose 2 answers.

[A] art

[B] arrogance

[C] sadness

[D] truth

Academic Talk 3: History

🎧 **Track 18**

Directions: Now use your notes to help you answer the questions.

23 What is the lecture mainly about?

(A) customs of the New Year

(B) ancient agricultural rites

(C) changes in the calendar

(D) influence of the church on holidays

24 Where did the name of the first month come from?

(A) a pope

(B) a statue

(C) a god

(D) a river

25 What can be inferred about the earliest dates for the New Year?

(A) Without calendars, no one could decide on a set date.

(B) The dates were linked to important seasonal changes.

(C) New civilizations carried on the date of the previous civilization.

(D) New Year was never celebrated until it was assigned to January.

26 Listen to part of the talk again, and then answer the question. Why does the professor say this: 🎧

(A) to underscore that spring is a logical time to celebrate the New Year

(B) to prompt students to question the sense of those who changed the date

(C) to express uncertainty about the relationship of spring and the New Year

(D) to encourage students to participate in class discussion of the topic

27 According to the talk, which of the following is true of the New Year's holiday?

(A) It was not always celebrated on January 1st.

(B) It was first celebrated in Egypt.

(C) The Catholic Church supported New Year's as they did Christmas.

(D) It was only celebrated by agricultural societies in the past.

28 Listen to part of the talk again, and then answer the question. What does the professor mean when she says this: 🎧

    Ⓐ The people in the house would then have good luck all year long.

    Ⓑ Those in the house would have many friends visiting at midnight.

    Ⓒ The first person to enter the house would owe all the men money.

    Ⓓ The residents of the house looked forward to getting gifts all year.

Academic Talk 4: Physics

🎧 **Track 19**

Directions: Now use your notes to help you answer the questions.

29 What is the main topic of the lecture?

    Ⓐ The role of physics in the development of batteries

    Ⓑ The invention of the dry cell or flashlight battery

    Ⓒ How to increase the power available from batteries

    Ⓓ How batteries produce portable power

30 What does the professor imply?

    Ⓐ Batteries are essential in spite of their high environmental cost.

    Ⓑ Batteries will never be cost-effective for use in electric vehicles.

    Ⓒ The convenience of batteries justifies their higher cost.

    Ⓓ The cost of batteries needs to be reduced.

31 Listen to part of the talk again, and then answer the question. Why does the professor refer to givers and takers?

    Ⓐ to make an abstract concept easier to understand

    Ⓑ to find out if students have understood the lecture

    Ⓒ to correct a misunderstanding

    Ⓓ to summarize his conclusions so far

32 According to the professor, why is the dry cell battery better than earlier batteries?

    Ⓐ It is easier to transport.

    Ⓑ It uses less zinc.

    Ⓒ It is cheaper to manufacture.

    Ⓓ It is more powerful.

33 Why does the professor use the example of the water pipe?

(A) to introduce the work of James Watt

(B) to clarify the meaning of voltage and current

(C) to demonstrate that water can also provide power

(D) to show how current in a battery flows in only one direction

34 According to the lecture, which of the following are true of batteries?

Choose 3 answers.

A The only way to increase electrical power in a circuit is connect several batteries.

B The electrolyte in a battery does not have to be a liquid.

C Power depends on both current and voltage.

D Three different materials are needed to create a battery.

E Batteries stop working because the electrolyte gets used up.

SPEAKING SECTION

Directions: In this section, you will be asked to respond to a variety of tasks and topics. There are six tasks. Respond to each task as completely as you can, always speaking clearly.

For tasks 1 and 2, you will speak about topics that are familiar to you. Your responses will be graded on your ability to speak about the topics clearly.

For tasks 3 and 4, you will be asked to read a short text. For each task, you will be asked a question about what you have read and heard. You will need to use information from the text and the talk to answer the questions. Your responses will be graded on your ability to speak clearly and accurately about what you have read and heard.

For tasks 5 and 6, you will hear part of a dialogue or an academic talk. For each task, you will then answer a question about what you have heard. Your responses will be graded on your ability to speak clearly and accurately about what you have heard.

You are allowed to take notes during the reading and listening. You are allowed to use your notes to help you respond. Read the directions for each task closely.

For each task, you will be given a short time to prepare your response. You will be given a certain amount of time to speak. Use a watch or clock to time yourself.

Task 1

Directions: Task One. For this task, you will be asked to speak about a topic that is familiar to you. You will hear a question. You will then have 15 seconds to prepare your response and 45 seconds to speak.

 Track 20

Describe a place you like to visit and explain why you like it. Include details and give examples to support your explanation.

> 15 seconds to prepare
> 45 seconds to speak

Task 2

Directions: Task Two. For this task, you will give your opinion about a topic that is familiar to you. You will hear a question. You will then have 15 seconds to prepare your response and 45 seconds to speak.

 Track 21

Some people like to socialize with a group of people. Other people like to spend time alone. Which way do you prefer to spend your free time? Include details and examples in your explanation.

> 15 seconds to prepare
> 45 seconds to speak

Task 3

Directions: Task Three. For this task, you will read a short text and then listen to a dialogue about the same topic. You will hear a question about what you have read and heard. You will then have 30 seconds to prepare your response and 60 seconds to speak.

Eastern State University is planning to change its parking policy. Read the announcement about the change from the Department of Parking Management. You will have 45 seconds to read the announcement. Begin reading now.

An Announcement from the Department of Parking Management

Eastern State University has announced a new parking policy, which will go into effect in September 2017. This policy is intended to ensure that the very limited number of parking spaces available on campus are allocated as fairly as possible. Up to now, preference was given to faculty and staff and then to commuting students. Any remaining parking spaces were offered to students living on campus on the basis of seniority. Beginning with the coming academic year, the university will give out parking spaces by means of a lottery. Details about the lottery are available on the DPM website.

 Track 22

The woman expresses her opinion about a new university policy. State her opinion and explain the reasons she gives for holding that opinion.

> 30 seconds to prepare
>
> 60 seconds to speak

Task 4

Directions: Task Four. For this task, you will read a short text and then hear a talk about the same topic. You will hear a question about what you have read and heard. After you hear the question, you will then have 30 seconds to prepare your response and 60 seconds to speak.

Now read the passage about the British Corn Law. You have 45 seconds to read the passage. Begin reading now.

The Corn Law

While Great Britain fought the Napoleonic Wars with France from 1803 to 1815, it had not been possible for the English to import corn and other cereals from Europe. This led to higher bread prices and to more British landowners planting wheat. When the war with France ended in 1815, the landowners feared that cheaper imported grains would affect their profits. So Parliament, dominated by landowners, introduced legislation that became known as the Corn Law. The purpose of the law was to continue to regulate the importing of cereals and protect the profits of domestic farmers and landowners. The law stated that cereals could not be imported into Britain until the domestic price reached 80 shillings a quarter bushel. This meant that the cost of cereals and bread were kept artificially high.

Track 23

> The professor discusses the Corn Law. Using information from the lecture and the reading, explain why the Corn Law was enacted, and why some people opposed it.
>
> | 30 seconds to prepare |
> | --- |
> | 60 seconds to speak |

Task 5

Directions: Task Five. For this task, you will listen to a dialogue. You will hear a question about it. You will then have 20 seconds to prepare your response and 60 seconds to speak.

 Track 24

> The woman tries to persuade the man to do something. Say what she tries to persuade him to do and explain the reasons she gives.
>
> | 20 seconds to prepare |
> | --- |
> | 60 seconds to speak |

Task 6

Directions: Task Six. For this task, you will hear a short academic talk. You will hear a question about it. You will then have 20 seconds to prepare your response and 60 seconds to speak.

 Track 25

> Using points and examples from the talk, explain how economic factors contributed to the Harlem Renaissance in New York City in the early 1900s.
>
> | 20 seconds to prepare |
> | --- |
> | 60 seconds to speak |

WRITING SECTION

Directions: You will need to listen to track 26 for this section.

This section is designed to measure your ability to write in English. There are two tasks.

For the first task, you will read a short text and listen to an academic talk. You will answer a question about what you have read and heard. For the second task, you will use your knowledge and experience to answer a question.

Task 1

Directions: For this task, you will have 3 minutes to read a short text. You may take notes if you wish. Then you will hear an academic talk on the same topic. You may take notes while you listen.

You will then read a question that asks about the relationship between the text and the talk. You will have 20 minutes to write a response. Using information from the text and talk, answer the question as completely as you can. You will not be asked to give your opinion. You will be able to review the text while you write. You may use your notes to help you write your response.

You should try to write 150 words or more. Your response will be graded on the quality, completeness, and accuracy of your writing. If you finish early, you may move on to the second task.

In this question, you will read a short passage and then listen to a talk on the same topic. You will then have 20 minutes to write an answer to the question that follows, using your notes and the written passage for reference.

You now have 3 minutes to read the passage. After you read the passage, listen to the talk.

There are different theories that attempt to explain how people learn a second language, two of which are the "nativist" theory and the "environmentalist" theory. The nativist theory proposes that the process of learning a second language is the same as the process of learning a first language. According to nativism, humans have an innate biological function that allows them to process and acquire language, regardless of whether it is a first language learned as an infant, or a second language learned later in life. Two proprietors of this branch are Noel Chomsky and Eric Lenneberg.

In 1965, Chomsky proposed that all children utilize an innate process, or an internal "language acquisition device" to learn their first language. Chomsky hypothesized that when humans are born, they are born with basic knowledge of the rules and structures of a language. Chomsky believed that humans learn the complex rules of their mother tongue at a very rapid pace and that this pace cannot be attributed to external language input. Therefore, it must be due to a biological function.

In 1967, Lenneberg also proposed that language acquisition is an innate process that allows humans to learn a language best between the ages of two years old and puberty. This theory, called the "Critical Period Hypothesis," suggests that upon reaching puberty, the two hemispheres of the brain begin functioning independently, causing a neurological change that makes learning new languages nearly impossible.

In essence, Chomsky and Lenneberg believed that humans have a special ability to acquire languages in their early years and that if this ability is not exercised during this period, they lose the ability to learn and process language.

 ## Track 26

Summarize the main points in the lecture you just heard, explaining how they cast doubt on the points made in the reading.

Task 2

For this task, you will be asked to write an essay in which you state, explain, and support your opinion on an issue. You will have 30 minutes to complete your essay.

You should try to write 300 words or more. Your essay will be graded on how well you use language, organize your essay, and develop your ideas.

> In your opinion, which modern invention or scientific discovery has affected society the most?

Use specific reasons and examples to support your answer.

Practice
Test 3

TEST DIRECTIONS

This test is designed to measure your ability to understand and to use English in an academic context. The test has four sections.

In the **Reading** section, you will read three passages and answer questions about them.

In the **Listening** section, you will listen to two dialogues and four talks and answer questions about them.

In the **Speaking** section, there are six tasks. The first two tasks ask you to speak based on your own personal experience. In the other four, you will read passages and/or listen to dialogues and talks, then speak based on what you have read and/or heard.

In the **Writing** section, there are two tasks. In the first task, you will read a passage, listen to a talk, then write based on what you have read and heard. The second task asks you to write based on your own personal experience and ideas.

There is a 10-minute break after the **Listening** section.

At the beginning of each section, there are directions that explain how to answer the questions or respond to the tasks in the section.

In the **Reading** and **Listening** sections, you should work carefully but quickly. You should try to answer every question to the best of your ability. Make an educated guess on questions that you are unsure of. In the **Speaking** and **Writing** sections, each task is separately timed. In each case, you should try to respond to the task as completely as possible in the given time.

READING SECTION

Directions: In this section of the test, you will read three passages. You will be tested on your ability to understand them by answering several questions on each passage.

While you read, you may take notes. You can then use your notes when answering questions.

Most questions are worth one point. Questions that are worth more than one point have a special note telling you how many total points they are worth.

You will have 60 minutes to read the three passages and answer all the questions. If you finish the questions before 60 minutes is up, you can go back and review your work in this section.

Passage 1

Acid Rain

Recently, the concentration of sulfur-containing compounds in the atmosphere has increased in urban and industrial environments. The problem originates with the burning of fossil fuels—such as coal, natural gas, and oil—in power plants for the purpose of making electricity. In the burning process, also called combustion, oxygen from the air combines with carbon and sulfur in the substance being burned to form gases called oxides. When sulfur is present in the fuel, reaction with oxygen produces sulfur dioxide (SO_2). In the United States, 80 percent of the sulfur dioxide in the atmosphere comes from power plants that burn coal or oil. The extent to which SO_2 emissions is a problem in the burning of coal and oil depends on the level of their sulfur concentrations.

In the atmosphere, SO_2 can be oxidized to sulfur trioxide (SO_3) by reaction with oxygen (O). When SO_3 dissolves in water, it produces sulfuric acid (H_2SO_4). Many of the environmental effects ascribed to SO_2 are actually due to the reaction product H_2SO_4. The sulfuric acid eventually returns to the ground by way of rain, snow, or fog; this phenomenon is known as acid rain.

Rainwater is naturally acidic and generally has a pH value in the range of 5 to 6. The term pH, which stands for potential of hydrogen, measures the acidity of a substance. The pH scale ranges from zero (the most acidic) to 14 (the most alkaline). A change of one unit on the pH scale represents a tenfold change in acidity. Living organisms generally thrive near pH 7, the neutral point, and function less successfully toward either end of the scale. When pH levels of rainwater drop below 5.6, the rainwater is considered acid rain.

The primary source of rainwater's natural acidity is carbon dioxide (CO_2), well known to us as the gas that we exhale. Carbon dioxide reacts with water to form carbonic acid (H_2CO_3). Acid rain, however, is more acidic than normal rainwater and typically has a pH of about 4. Its corrosive nature causes widespread damage to the environment and affects other parts of the ecological network.

In soil, acid rain dissolves and washes away useful nutrients needed by plants. This slows the plants' growth, especially that of affected trees. The acid rain also attacks trees by eating holes in the waxy coatings of their leaves and needles and leaving brown dead spots. If many such spots form, a tree loses some of its ability to make food through photosynthesis. Also, organisms that cause disease can infect the

K

tree through its injured leaves. Once weakened, trees are more vulnerable to other stresses, such as insect infestations, drought, and cold temperatures.

Acid rain can also release toxic substances that are naturally present in some soils, such as aluminum and mercury, freeing these toxins to pollute water or to poison plants that absorb them. In cities, acid pollutants accelerate natural wear on buildings and statues.

Water with a pH below 4.5 is unable to support wildlife. If one plant or animal population is adversely affected by acid rain, animals that feed on that organism may also suffer, and the entire ecosystem is likely to be affected. In the air, acids join with other chemicals to produce urban smog, which can irritate the lungs and make breathing difficult, especially for people who already have respiratory diseases.

Acid rain can best be curtailed by reducing the amount of sulfur dioxide released by power plants, vehicles, and factories. **A** The simplest ways to cut these emissions are to use less energy from fossil fuels and to lessen emissions of sulfur dioxide by switching to cleaner-burning fuels. **B** Using cleanable coals and low-sulfur fuels will enable electric-utility companies and other industrial businesses to lower their pollution emissions. **C** Auto-emission pollution can be reduced by using clean-burning fuels such as natural gas, which contains almost no sulfur, and is being used more often in vehicles. **D**

Unfortunately, natural gas and the less-polluting coals tend to be more expensive, and this puts them out of the reach of poorer nations.

1   The main source of acid rain-causing chemicals in the United States is

    (A) gasoline.

    (B) coal.

    (C) power plants.

    (D) factories.

2   Based on information in paragraph 2, which of the following best explains the term *acid rain*?

    (A) rain that contains excess sulfur trioxide

    (B) sulfur dioxide that is present in rain

    (C) rain that contains unhealthy levels of oxygen

    (D) rain that contains sulfuric acid

3   The word thrive in the passage is closest in meaning to

    (A) do well.

    (B) struggle.

    (C) survive.

    (D) give up.

4   The passage discusses the potential of hydrogen (pH) scale in paragraph 3 in order to

    (A) show how acidity can be present at healthy or unhealthy levels.

    (B) describe the relationship of acidity to the composition of acid rain.

    (C) explain how the sulfur content of acid rain is measured on a scale.

    (D) illustrate the negative consequences of high acid-content rain.

5   According to the passage, the acidity of normal rainwater comes from

    (A) sulfur dioxide.

    (B) a toxic gas in the atmosphere.

    (C) carbon dioxide.

    (D) the breathing of humans.

6   According to the passage, acid rain causes damage mainly by

    (A) creating an imbalance in the ecological system.

    (B) accelerating the natural erosion of buildings and statues.

    (C) producing urban smog and increased greenhouse gases.

    (D) increasing the pH level of water in ecosystems.

7   The word adversely in the passage is closest in meaning to

    (A) especially.

    (B) negatively.

    (C) fatally.

    (D) unusually.

8   The word curtailed in the passage is closest in meaning to

    (A) lessened.

    (B) solved.

    (C) exacerbated.

    (D) suspended.

9   All of the following would most likely reduce the amount of acid rain-causing chemicals EXCEPT

    (A) converting car engines to run on electricity.

    (B) using more solar and wind power.

    (C) installing sulfur dioxide filters on power plants.

    (D) drilling for new sources of fossil fuels.

10 Look at the four letters (**A**, **B**, **C**, and **D**) in the passage that show where the following sentence could be inserted.

For instance, some coal contains sulfur in a form that can be washed out easily before the coal is burned.

Where would the sentence best fit in the passage? Choose the letter for the square where this sentence should be added.

11 It can be inferred from the passage that acidity

    Ⓐ is always harmful to living systems.

    Ⓑ is a natural element in the ecosystem.

    Ⓒ originated with the industrial revolution.

    Ⓓ is unnatural in rainwater.

12 **Directions:** Below is an introductory sentence for a short summary of the passage. Complete the summary by choosing the THREE answer choices that express key ideas in the passage. Sentences that express ideas that are NOT in the passage or mention minor details do NOT belong in the summary. *This question is worth 2 points.*

Acid rain is a serious environmental problem affecting industrialized countries.

Answer Choices	
A. People with respiratory problems are particularly vulnerable to the negative health effects of acid rain.	D. The most effective way of reducing acid rain is to cut back on the use of fossil fuels, and to use cleaner fuel alternatives.
B. Acid rain is caused by the emission of sulfur dioxide, most of which comes from oil and coal-fueled power plants.	E. Acid rain hurts trees by damaging their leaves, which impedes their ability to manufacture food through photosynthesis.
C. Acid rain washes away soil and slows plant growth due to absorption of toxic substances that are released.	F. Sulfur dioxide reacts with oxygen in the atmosphere to produce sulfuric acid, which falls to the earth in the form of precipitation.

Passage 2

Samuel Adams and the Shot Heard Around the World

Though it was his cousin John Adams who would become the second president of the United States, Samuel Adams was no less important to the nation's history. He played an instrumental role in America's fight for independence. As the Boston representative to the Massachusetts General Court, Adams was so vocal in his criticism of the "Crown"—as the British government was known—that both

Parliament and British military governor General Thomas Gage attempted to bribe him into ceasing his attacks. Adams declined both offers and continued.

As Adams had warned, the British began to tax the colonies. First, in 1763 Parliament announced that taxes would be levied against the colonies and the funds would be used at the full discretion of the Crown. In May of 1765, they passed the "Quartering Act," requiring the colonists to provide shelter and ultimately housing for British Troops.

Although anti-British sentiment existed in the colonies, only one third of the population wanted independence from Britain. Sam Adams worked to rally public opinion against the Crown and is believed to have organized the protest that led to the Boston Massacre of March 5, 1770, in which British regulars shot and killed five colonists. The dead became instant martyrs for the cause of revolution advocated by Adams and his compatriots. Subsequent British actions would add more fuel to the fire.

In May of 1773, the British government removed all import taxes for the East India Company, which the Crown also subsidized. This meant that a half million pounds of below-market priced tea would flood the colonial marketplace and ruin local merchants. On the night of December 16, 1773, Adams and the Boston Whigs solved the problem by throwing 342 cases of tea into the ocean.

The "Boston Tea Party" was a direct challenge to England's authority. In response, on May 20, 1774, Parliament passed a series of laws known as the "Intolerable or Coercive Acts." The Administration of Justice Act stated that a British official could not be tried in a colonial court and must return to Britain for trial. The Massachusetts Government Act nullified the charter of the colonies making the British Governor sole manager of all government activities. The Acts also expanded the borders of the territory of Quebec, at the expense of the western portions of several American colonies, including Massachusetts.

After the Massachusetts Government Act of 1774 was passed and there was no longer a formal colonial government, Samuel Adams and John Hancock created the Massachusetts Provincial Congress. This was an illegal body and its existence disturbed the British Governor of Massachusetts. Adams and Hancock were now direct and personal challengers to Governor Thomas Gage's authority.

On April 11, 1774, Adams and Hancock met in Concord, Massachusetts, to discuss their circumstances. At the same time Governor Gage was ordered to send troops to Concord to take possession of the colonial militia's armament and gunpowder and to take Adams and Hancock into custody. Thanks to a good spy network, the colonials knew of Gage's plan for the April 19th march to Concord. The day before, Paul Revere and William Dawes rode toward Concord warning the countryside of the upcoming troop movement.

While Adams and Hancock remained in hiding, 77 citizen soldiers, also known as "Minutemen," assembled at Lexington Green. Under Gage's command, Major John Pitcairn led the first 200 British Grenadiers toward the American patriots. Lexington Militia Captain John Parker, seeing how dramatically outnumbered his men were, ordered the soldiers to disperse. Before the men could run for the woods, a shot rang out. It is unknown who fired the shot, but the British then fired, killing and wounding almost 20 Minutemen.

British troops then proceeded to Concord. They were encountered 300 to 400 armed colonists at the North Bridge. The 120 British troops fired and—for the first time—the colonists fired back, killing British soldiers. **A** The colonial soldiers used hit, run, and hide tactics similar to how Native Americans fought battles. **B** And as a result, as outnumbered as they were overall, the American colonists forced the British to order a retreat back to Concord center. **C** The British officer in command, knowing of the danger his troops faced from this unorthodox form of warfare ordered a retreat to return to Boston. **D** Thus colonial militiamen fired the "shot heard around the world," heralding the start of the American Revolutionary War, a war that would not only change North America, but also the world.

13 The word ceasing in the passage is closest in meaning to

  (A) strengthening.
  (B) decreasing.
  (C) stopping.
  (D) softening.

14 According to the passage, before the Revolution, American colonists

  (A) were almost unanimous in supporting independence.
  (B) were almost all opposed to independence.
  (C) were more in favor of staying under British rule.
  (D) were apathetic about independence.

15 Which of the following sentences most closely expresses the important information in the highlighted sentence in the passage?

  (A) Future deeds of the Crown would further provoke the colonists' anger.
  (B) These past British acts would make war almost inevitable.
  (C) Later British actions included the use of explosives.
  (D) British actions to come would be considerably more violent.

16 According to the passage, the Boston Tea Party was

  (A) a political party formed to oppose British rule.
  (B) a response to low-priced tea coming into colonial markets.
  (C) a nighttime meeting of colonial revolutionaries.
  (D) a celebration of the first harvest of American-grown tea.

17 According to the passage, all of the following were aspects of the "Intolerable or Coercive Acts" EXCEPT

    (A) placing British officials above American courts of law.

    (B) moving the border of some colonies to the east.

    (C) the abolition of self-government for the colonies.

    (D) requiring colonists to give lodging to British soldiers.

18 It can be inferred from the passage that Paul Revere and William Dawes were

    (A) British spies for General Gage.

    (B) members of the colonial militia.

    (C) Massachusetts Provincial Congressmen.

    (D) important men from Concord.

19 The word disperse in the passage is closest in meaning to

    (A) march forward.

    (B) surrender.

    (C) open fire.

    (D) disband.

20 Look at the four letters (**A**, **B**, **C**, and **D**) in the passage that show where the following sentence could be inserted.

This strategy of guerilla warfare proved to be highly effective.

Where would the sentence best fit in the passage? Choose the letter for the square where this sentence should be added.

21 The word unorthodox in paragraph 9 is closest in meaning to

    (A) atypical.

    (B) structured.

    (C) sacrilegious.

    (D) brutal.

22 Why does the author use the expression "the shot heard around the world"?

    (A) to emphasize the importance of the battles at Lexington and Concord

    (B) to introduce a new idea about the American Revolution

    (C) to contrast the size of the American and British forces

    (D) to summarize Britain's reaction to the battles at Lexington and Concord

23 Which of the following statements could describe the author's opinion about the beginning of the American Revolution?

(A) The battles of Lexington and Concord had global significance.

(B) The colonists initiated the war with Great Britain.

(C) The British should have been able to end the colonial rebellion easily.

(D) The colonists' grievances were exaggerated.

24 According to the passage, Sam Adams contributed to the American Revolution mainly by

(A) leading the colonial army in acts of rebellion.

(B) organizing the Boston Tea Party.

(C) establishing the Massachusetts Provincial Congress.

(D) consistently generating popular support for the cause.

25 **Directions:** Find the phrases in the answer choices list that relate to the British or the colonists. Write your answers in the appropriate place. TWO of the answer choices will NOT match either category. *This question is worth 4 points.*

Answer Choices	Actions taken by the British
A. Offered bribes to Samuel Adams	
B. Created Massachusetts Provincial Government	
C. Allied themselves with Native Americans	**Actions taken by the colonists**
D. Removed import taxes from East India Company	
E. Dumped tea into the Boston Harbor	
F. Formed citizen militias	
G. Passed the Massachusetts Government Act	
H. Closed the border between Canada and the colonies	
I. Used hit-and-run military tactics	

Passage 3

Attention Deficit/Hyperactivity Disorder

In the past, Attention Deficit/Hyperactivity Disorder (ADHD) was defined by the presence of motor restlessness, or excessive activity. Although hyperactivity was associated with impulsivity and attention deficits, the latter were never emphasized. Some past labels used in place of the more modern term ADHD, such as hyperkinesis, attest to this oversight. Today however, ADHD focuses not only upon motor activity, but also upon attention deficits, which are then associated with hyperactivity.

ADHD has a complex etiology, or set of causes, although most psychiatrists ascribe it to biological factors. While evidence supports the hypothesis that ADHD may be genetically transmitted, research has yet to identify the vehicle of transmission. Other possible causes that have been cited include brain dysfunction, and complications experienced during pregnancy and at birth. In addition, there have been studies examining the link between ADHD and diet, namely sugar. However, diet has not been found to play an important causative role.

In order to be classified as ADHD, an individual must display the following diagnostic features. First, the onset of the disorder must occur before the age of seven. This can sometimes prove difficult, as children below the age of five vary greatly in their development and thus symptoms may be difficult to identify. Second, the symptoms must be present for at least six months. Third, the symptoms must be found in at least two different surroundings, like home, school, or work. Finally, the inattention and/or hyperactivity needs to be more than what one would normally expect from an individual at a similar stage of development. The issue of normative development is often controversial because its boundaries can be so unclear. In diagnosing ADHD, mental health professionals must be sensitive to differences in age, culture, and gender.

ADHD consists of three subtypes. The subtypes are used to identify the dominant behavioral patterns that are indicated in their titles. The three subtypes, as noted in the Diagnostic and Statistical Manual IV (DSM) are: Predominantly* Inattentive, Predominantly Hyperactive-Impulsive, and Combined Type. The first subtype, Predominantly Inattentive, focuses on different aspects of attention. Individuals in this category may shift from task to task without finishing one or the other, make careless mistakes, and not listen to others. This may lead to frequent conversational shifts and inattention to detail. An individual's sustained attention, which examines the ability to focus on a task over time, and selective attention, which explores the ability to focus on a relevant task or stimulus without being distracted by unrelated elements, are often analyzed. Individuals with ADHD-Predominantly Inattentive tend to have fewer behavioral problems than those individuals with ADHD-Hyperactive-Impulsive.

On the other hand, the second subtype, Predominantly Hyperactive-Impulsive, emphasizes motor movement and impatience, concerning issues of motivation and self-regulation. This subtype is often seen at its earlier stages and then often progresses into the Combined Type. Individuals who exhibit this subtype may demonstrate difficulty remaining seated, fidgetiness, difficulty awaiting one's turn, and disorganized and haphazard behavior. Those with this subtype always appear to be on the move and show the greatest difficulty with tasks that are sedentary or highly structured.

The final subtype, the Combined Type, is the most common. It includes inattention, hyperactivity, and impulsivity. It is associated with being in constant motion, not following through on requests, getting sidetracked, interrupting, inability to participate in organized sports, and impulsivity impairing social interactions. The Combined Type includes a number of behaviors found in the two subtypes previously discussed, and thus widely affects functioning.

The treatment an individual receives for ADHD may vary. Methods used include Cognitive Behavioral Therapy (CBT), pharmacological treatment, individual counseling, and parent training. **A** In the U.S., the most popular form of treatment is pharmacological, or the use of medication. However, while research has found it to be effective in reducing impulsivity and increasing attention, there is still concern over side effects and the inability of medication to help all children. **B** Alternative treatments like behavioral interventions and CBT have been tried. **C** Unfortunately, they are only successful in certain domains, and the positive results are nowhere near as impressive as those found with the use of stimulant medication. **D**

predominantly: mostly or mainly

26 The author mentions the term *hyperkinesis* in paragraph 1 in order to

    (A) show how in the past people had a more narrow view of ADHD.

    (B) provide an example of a typical manifestation of ADHD.

    (C) demonstrate the role excited vision plays in ADHD.

    (D) suggest that ADHD was thought to only consist of a lack of attention.

27 Which of the following sentences most closely expresses the important information in the highlighted sentence in the passage?

    (A) Research indicates that ADHD may be passed on genetically, although it has not been determined precisely how.

    (B) Though they are uncertain about whether ADHD has a genetic origin, scientists are confident that they will discover its means of transmission.

    (C) Research has proven the theory that ADHD is spread genetically, but the spread of the disorder remains a mystery.

    (D) Research has determined how ADHD is spread, although it has not verified whether it has a genetic origin.

28 According to the passage, all of the following are thought to be major factors in the development of ADHD EXCEPT

   (A) genes.

   (B) brain disorder.

   (C) prenatal problems.

   (D) diet.

29 Based on the information in paragraph 3, all of the following would support a diagnosis of ADHD EXCEPT

   (A) a child showing symptoms of ADHD before age seven.

   (B) ADHD symptoms that are present for three months.

   (C) symptoms of the disorder observed at home and school.

   (D) inability to sit still in an 18-year-old.

30 The word onset in the passage is closest in meaning to

   (A) symptoms.

   (B) development.

   (C) peak.

   (D) features.

31 It can be inferred from the passage that children's normative development

   (A) is essentially the same regardless of culture and gender.

   (B) is impossible to determine accurately due to genetics.

   (C) varies depending on biological and cultural factors.

   (D) depends on the income of their parents.

32 According to the passage, all of the following are primary indicators of the Predominantly Hyperactive-Impulsive subtype EXCEPT

   (A) an inability to stay seated for an extended period of time.

   (B) making careless mistakes.

   (C) difficulty participating in organized sports.

   (D) impatience.

33 According to the passage, ADHD could best be described as

(A) an inherited physical disorder best treated with surgical intervention.

(B) a mental condition usually treated through psychiatric counseling.

(C) an emotional disorder characterized by impulsiveness and impatience.

(D) a biological disorder characterized by inattentiveness and hyperactivity.

34 The word sidetracked in the passage is closest in meaning to

(A) lost.

(B) in trouble.

(C) distracted.

(D) aggressive.

35 Look at the four letters (**A**, **B**, **C**, and **D**) in the passage that show where the following sentence could be inserted.

Critics argue that this type of treatment simply supplies a quick and easy answer to the problems faced by many schools and parents.

Where would the sentence best fit in the passage? Choose the letter for the square where this sentence should be added.

36 **Directions:** Below is an introductory sentence for a short summary of the passage. Complete the summary by choosing the THREE answer choices that express key ideas in the passage. Sentences that express ideas that are NOT in the passage or mention minor details do NOT belong in the summary. *This question is worth 2 points.*

Attention Deficit/Hyperactivity Disorder is a condition characterized by impulsive behavior and difficulties maintaining concentration.

Answer Choices	
A. To be diagnosed with ADHD, a person must show symptoms in different settings before the age of seven.	D. Treatment of ADHD may include counseling and skills training, although in America there is a preference for pharmacological remedies.
B. Some psychiatrists suspect that sugar and other dietary factors may contribute to ADHD.	E. The causal factors of ADHD are thought to be largely biological; scientists speculate that it may derive from genes or natal conditions.
C. The disorder consists of three subtypes: Predominantly Inattentive, Predominantly Hyperactive-Impulsive, and Combined.	F. Combined type ADHD involves the exhibition of both hyperactive and inattentive behaviors and is the least common type.

LISTENING SECTION

Directions: In this section of the test, you will hear dialogues and academic talks, and you will be tested on your ability to understand them. You will hear each dialogue and academic talk only once, and then answer some questions after each is finished. The questions ask about the main idea, supporting details, and the way the speakers use language. Answer each question based on what is stated or implied by the speakers. You cannot go back to a question once you have answered it. Answer every question in the order that it appears.

While you listen, you may take notes. You can then use your notes when answering questions.

You will see the following headphones icon next to some questions: This icon indicates that you will hear part of the dialogue or academic talk repeated for the question.

Most questions are worth one point. Questions that are worth more than one point have a special note telling you how many total points they are worth.

You will be given 20 minutes to answer all the questions in this section. This does not include the time to listen to the dialogues and academic talks.

Dialogue 1

 Track 27

Directions: Now use your notes to help you answer the questions.

1 How does the professor know the student?

    (A) He recently read an article she had published.

    (B) She worked for him the previous semester.

    (C) He heard about her from one of his colleagues.

    (D) She was a student in one of his classes.

2 Why does the professor think the student could work well with him?

    (A) She is available every day.

    (B) She is bilingual and can help him translate.

    (C) She is very precise in her research.

    (D) She knows how to use several spreadsheet programs.

3 What does the professor want the student to do first?

    (A) Check databases for journal articles.

    (B) Enter data from questionnaires.

    (C) Distribute 200 questionnaires.

    (D) Read his book prospectus on test taking.

4 What can be inferred about most of the work the student will have to do?

    Ⓐ It has to be done on a computer.

    Ⓑ It will be tedious.

    Ⓒ It will involve talking to bilingual students.

    Ⓓ It will be done mainly on the weekends.

5 Listen to part of the dialogue again, and then answer the question. What does the professor imply when he says this: 🎧

    Ⓐ that the student is not qualified for the job

    Ⓑ that the student should look for a research position

    Ⓒ that the student might not have time for the job

    Ⓓ that the student has time now that she lives on campus

Dialogue 2

🎧 **Track 28**

Directions: Now use your notes to help you answer the questions.

6 What is the student's main concern with the course he wants to drop?

    Ⓐ He thinks there are too many assignments.

    Ⓑ He thinks his fellow students are not taking their work seriously.

    Ⓒ He wants to do extra work because he failed the midterm exam.

    Ⓓ He feels the course is not being as well taught as it should be.

7 Why did the student think the midterm exam was unusual?

    Ⓐ It covered only four points from the professor's lectures.

    Ⓑ It included material that was never covered in class.

    Ⓒ It was not mandatory.

    Ⓓ It was 65 percent of the final grade.

8 Why does the advisor say the student can drop the course now?

    Ⓐ because the student agreed to audit the course instead

    Ⓑ because he will substitute the course with another

    Ⓒ because he can do so without being penalized

    Ⓓ because he is an honors student and has the privilege

9   What can be inferred as the main reason the student asked about dropping the course?

   (A) He realized he would spoil his 4.0 GPA.

   (B) He has a habit of not finished what he started.

   (C) He just learned the course is not a requirement.

   (D) He wanted to file a formal complaint about the professor.

10 Listen to part of the dialogue again, and then answer the question. What does the advisor mean?

   (A) The student obviously works hard in his courses.

   (B) The student cannot get A grades all the time.

   (C) The student needs to reduce his working hours.

   (D) The student should try harder in the class.

Academic Talk 1: Women's Studies

🎧 **Track 29**

Directions: Now use your notes to help you answer the questions.

11 What is the talk mainly about?

   (A) Historical background of the Indian women's movement

   (B) The impact of the women's movement on government

   (C) Comparisons between the U.S. and Indian constitutions

   (D) Parallels between rural and urban women in India

12 How did Indian village women show their support for demonstrators?

   (A) They represented their villages at conferences.

   (B) They participated in women's cultural presentations.

   (C) They made loud noises using household objects.

   (D) They stopped doing chores for their husbands and sons.

13 What can be inferred about the Indian women's movement from the 1970s to 1980s?

   (A) It solved all the social problems facing Indian women up to that time.

   (B) It brought Indian women together

   (C) It paralleled the U.S. feminist movement on exactly the same issues.

   (D) It initiated a global feminist movement supported by the United Nations.

14 Listen to part of the talk again, and then answer the question. Why does the professor say this:

    Ⓐ to ask permission to discuss a different topic

    Ⓑ to prompt students to pay attention to the next point

    Ⓒ to compare and contrast two countries side by side

    Ⓓ to introduce a point that is not under discussion

15 Listen to part of the talk again, and then answer the question. What does the student mean when she says this: 🎧

    Ⓐ She believes it is time for the women's movement to change.

    Ⓑ She also used to hold the belief she is describing.

    Ⓒ She once was an angry demonstrator.

    Ⓓ She agrees with those perceptions.

16 In the talk, the professor describes a number of facts that are part of the Indian women's movement. Indicate which of the following were mentioned in the talk.

	Yes	No
A. Marches through villages		
B. Effective use of the media		
C. Theatrical presentations		
D. Concerns over land rights		
E. Elections to political office		

Academic Talk 2: Film Studies

🎧 **Track 30**

Directions: Now use your notes to help you answer the questions.

17 What is the talk mainly about?

    Ⓐ the ways to manipulate a film viewer's emotions

    Ⓑ the complicated process of editing a film

    Ⓒ the lack of respect given to film editors

    Ⓓ the blending of sound and image in film

18 According to the talk, which of the following are two aspects of a film editor's job?

Choose 2 answers.

A helping the director with his or her ideas

B putting images and sound together

C influencing how an audience sees a movie

D making sure the actors look good

19 What can be inferred about the editor's job?

A It is very detail-oriented.

B It is easier than other film jobs.

C It is often awarded top honors.

D It is incredibly frustrating.

20 Listen to part of the talk again, and then answer the question. What is the purpose of the professor asking this question: 🎧

A to encourage students to question the statement she has just made

B to cue students that she will support her point with good reasons

C to question the idea that editing is a vital component of the film process

D to counteract skepticism that she sees in the student's expressions

21 Listen to part of the talk again, and then answer the question. What are the students implying?

A They cannot agree on what the word *manipulation* means.

B They agree that each had a good point about manipulation.

C They are contradicting each other in explaining manipulation.

D They think the professor has the right idea about manipulation.

22 Listen to part of the talk again, and then answer the question. Why does the professor say this: 🎧

A The scene is showing a boxing match.

B The scene might frighten people.

C The scene could have an emotional effect.

D The scene was edited poorly.

Academic Talk 3: Music

🎧 **Track 31**

Directions: Now use your notes to help you answer the questions.

23 What is the talk mainly about?

    (A) a singer who writes songs about the importance of water in society

    (B) songs that express women's anger against society

    (C) a singer whose songs deal with emotional reactions to life

    (D) songs that focus on a fast-paced lifestyle

24 What can be inferred about the singer's attitude toward nature?

    (A) She feels it is unpredictably destructive.

    (B) She feels its changes come in predictable waves.

    (C) She feels thinks it helps people to converse with each other.

    (D) She feels it is a source of personal healing.

25 Listen to part of the talk again, and then answer the question. Why does the professor say this: 🎧

    (A) to indicate he is using a different meaning for the word *crash*.

    (B) to encourage students to look up the definition of *crash*.

    (C) to question the singer's original meaning of *crash*.

    (D) to justify his misuse of the word *crash* in this context.

26 Listen to part of the talk again, and then answer the question. What does the student mean when he says this: 🎧

    (A) He thinks his classmate is completely wrong.

    (B) He is trying to get his classmate to change her mind.

    (C) He is reminding his classmate there's more to consider.

    (D) He forgot the point his classmate was making.

27 Listen to part of the talk again, and then answer the question. Why does the professor say this: 🎧

    (A) He is about to start singing for the students.

    (B) He is about to read from a new set of notes.

    (C) He wants the students to talk about something personal.

    (D) He is about to share his thoughts with the class.

28 In the lecture, the professor discusses several themes covered in the songs. Indicate which of the following themes are considered by the singer.

	Yes	No
A. Gender issues		
B. Fast-paced living		
C. Loneliness		
D. Death		
E. Environmental pollution		

Academic Talk 4: History

Track 32

Directions: Now use your notes to help you answer the questions.

29 What is the talk mainly about?

- Ⓐ Jefferson's presidency
- Ⓑ French perceptions of Virginia
- Ⓒ Jefferson's philosophy of government
- Ⓓ Jefferson's interpretation of his home state

30 What is the logical progression of Jefferson's description of Virginia?

- Ⓐ from physical to philosophical
- Ⓑ from ancient to modern
- Ⓒ from animals to people
- Ⓓ from small towns to large cities

31 How do the two parts of Jefferson's book reflect his personality?

- Ⓐ They show he has not traveled widely throughout the state.
- Ⓑ They show he is a scientist above all other occupations.
- Ⓒ They show that he is objective as well as subjective.
- Ⓓ They show that he likes to argue both sides of a subject.

32 Listen to part of the talk again, and then answer the question. What does the professor mean when he says this: 🎧

- Ⓐ He thinks Jefferson presents full details of each topic he addresses.
- Ⓑ He thinks Jefferson passes over the topics very broadly.
- Ⓒ He thinks Jefferson was disorganized in his presentation of lists.
- Ⓓ He thinks Jefferson included too many facts and details in his book.

33 Listen to part of the talk again, and then answer the question. Why does the professor say this: 🎧

    Ⓐ to tell the students that he will need to leave the class early

    Ⓑ to encourage the students to think out the question themselves

    Ⓒ to test students' ability to infer concepts from their notes

    Ⓓ to suggest that Jefferson did not know much about biology

34 Listen to part of the talk again, and then answer the question. What does the professor imply when he says this: 🎧

    Ⓐ He thinks Jefferson says nothing new in his conclusion.

    Ⓑ He thinks Jefferson presents the most impressive material at the end.

    Ⓒ He thinks Jefferson tries to pack in a lot of information at the end.

    Ⓓ He thinks Jefferson holds back information so he can write another book.

SPEAKING SECTION

Directions: In this section, you will be asked to respond to a variety of tasks and topics. There are six tasks. Respond to each task as completely as you can, always speaking clearly.

For tasks 1 and 2, you will speak about topics that are familiar to you. Your responses will be graded on your ability to speak about the topics clearly.

For tasks 3 and 4, you will be asked to read a short text. For each task, you will be asked a question about what you have read and heard. You will need to use information from the text and the talk to answer the questions. Your responses will be graded on your ability to speak clearly and accurately about what you have read and heard.

For tasks 5 and 6, you will hear part of a dialogue or an academic talk. For each task, you will then answer a question about what you have heard. Your responses will be graded on your ability to speak clearly and accurately about what you have heard.

You are allowed to take notes during the reading and listening. You are allowed to use your notes to help you respond. Read the directions for each task closely.

For each task, you will be given a short time to prepare your response. You will be given a certain amount of time to speak. Use a watch or clock to time yourself.

Task 1

Directions: Task One. For this task, you will be asked to speak about a topic that is familiar to you. You will hear a question. You will then have 15 seconds to prepare your response and 45 seconds to speak.

 Track 33

Talk about a challenge that you've had to face and explain how you managed to overcome it. Include details and examples in your response.

> 15 seconds to prepare
>
> 45 seconds to speak

Task 2

Directions: Task Two. For this task, you will give your opinion about a topic that is familiar to you. You will hear a question. You will then have 15 seconds to prepare your response and 45 seconds to speak.

 Track 34

Some people want to be friends with their parents. Others prefer to maintain the more traditional parent-child relationship. Which approach do you favor and why? Give details and examples to support your choice.

> 15 seconds to prepare
>
> 45 seconds to speak

Task 3

Directions: Task Three. For this task, you will read a short text and then listen to a dialogue about the same topic. You will hear a question about what you have read and heard. You will then have 30 seconds to prepare your response and 60 seconds to speak.

North Park University is planning to build new athletic facilities. Read the announcement about the plans from the Office of Alumni Relations. You will have 45 seconds to read the announcement. Begin reading now.

An Announcement from the Office of Alumni Relations

North Park University is pleased to announce that construction of a new sports facility will commence this spring. Among the features of the new state-of-the-art sports complex will be a basketball court and an Olympic-size swimming pool. The new center, which will be used for competitions as well as for recreation, is made possible by a generous grant from Thomas C. Watson, a 1969 alumnus of the university. It is thanks to the generous support of alumni like Mr. Watson, that we can make improvements to the campus for the benefit of the whole university community.

 Track 35

The man expresses his opinion about the announcement made by the alumni office. State his opinion and explain the reasons he gives for holding that opinion.

> 30 seconds to prepare
> 60 seconds to speak

Task 4

Directions: Task Four. For this task, you will read a short text and then hear a talk about the same topic. You will hear a question about what you have read and heard. After you hear the question, you will then have 30 seconds to prepare your response and 60 seconds to speak.

Now read the passage about wolves. You have 45 seconds to read the passage. Begin reading now.

Wolves in Yellowstone Park

Wolves once roamed the North American continent from Mexico to the Arctic Circle. However, by 1973, when they were placed on the endangered species list, hunting and trapping had eliminated them from every U.S. state except Alaska and Minnesota. Even the massive Yellowstone National Park was no longer home to wolves. That changed in 1995 when 14 wolves were reintroduced to the park. Though environmentalists cheered the return of this natural predator to the park, ranchers and farmers whose lands abutted the park protested. They claimed that the wolves would leave the park to prey on their herds. The demanded the right to protect their property and animals from wolves. They even went to court to demand that the wolves be removed.

Track 36

The professor talks about the results of wolves being brought back to Yellowstone National Park. Explain what those results are and how those results are contrary to what people living near the park expected.

> 30 seconds to prepare
>
> 60 seconds to speak

Task 5

Directions: Task Five. For this task, you will listen to a dialogue. You will hear a question about it. You will then have 20 seconds to prepare your response and 60 seconds to speak.

 Track 37

The students discuss two solutions to the man's problem. Describe the problem. Then state which of the two solutions you prefer and why.

> 20 seconds to prepare
>
> 60 seconds to speak

Task 6

Directions: Task Six. For this task, you will hear a short academic talk. You will hear a question about it. You will then have 20 seconds to prepare your response and 60 seconds to speak.

 Track 38

Using points and examples from the talk, explain why Gideon's case was important and what values are reflected in the Supreme Court's decision.

> 20 seconds to prepare
>
> 60 seconds to speak

WRITING SECTION

Directions: You will need to listen to Track 39 for this section.

This section is designed to measure your ability to write in English. There are two tasks.

For the first task, you will read a short text and listen to an academic talk. You will answer a question about what you have read and heard. For the second task, you will use your knowledge and experience to answer a question.

Task 1

Directions: For this task, you will have 3 minutes to read a short text. You may take notes if you wish. Then you will hear an academic talk on the same topic. You may take notes while you listen.

You will then read a question that asks about the relationship between the text and the talk. You will have 20 minutes to write a response. Using information from the text and talk, answer the question as completely as you can. You will not be asked to give your opinion. You will be able to review the text while you write. You may use your notes to help you write your response.

You should try to write 150 words or more. Your response will be graded on the quality, completeness, and accuracy of your writing. If you finish early, you may move on to the second task.

In this question, you will read a short passage and then listen to a talk on the same topic. You will then have 20 minutes to write an answer to the question that follows, using your notes and the written passage for reference.

You now have 3 minutes to read the passage. After you read the passage, listen to the talk.

> On February 15th, 1898, the USS *Maine* sank off the coast of Havana, Cuba. More than two hundred soldiers and officers on board died as a result of an explosion, which many historians see as the catalyst to the ensuing Spanish-American War, waged between the United States and Spain.
>
> While the cause of the blast is still unknown, we do know that this was the first time the U.S. media asserted its power over the American public in the effort to sway public opinion against the Spanish. Hours after the sinking of the ship, journalist William Hearst's *New York Journal* created an anti-Spanish outcry by publishing the headline, T_{HE} W_{ARSHIP} *M_{AINE}* W_{AS} S_{PLIT IN} T_{WO} B_{Y AN} E_{NEMY'S} S_{ECRET} I_{NFERNAL} M_{ACHINE}! Immediately, the American public began to blame Spain for the explosion, and the sensationalist, "yellow" journalism that Hearst and fellow newsman Joseph Pulitzer had been perfecting for 10 years prior to the 1898 event, took up a powerful place in history.
>
> Pulitzer and Hearst had already been reporting on events involving General Weyler, a Spanish general in Cuba, blowing them completely out of proportion. In one famous story, a Hearst photographer in Cuba told the publisher that all was quiet in the country, to which Hearst replied, "You furnish the pictures and I'll furnish the war." This might seem overblown in today's world, but Hearst's papers had the power to influence public opinion in ways that no others had before him.

"Yellow journalism" is a term used to refer to journalism and newspapers that used provocative titles to attract attention, but very little factual data. "Yellow journalism" was not new in 1898, but it did play a large role in ensuring public support for the Spanish-American War. Without the influence of Hearst and Pulitzer, who knows if the conflict would ever have come to pass?

 Track 39

Summarize the points made in the talk you just heard, explaining how they cast doubt on the points made in the reading.

Task 2

For this task, you will be asked to write an essay in which you state, explain, and support your opinion on an issue. You will have 30 minutes to complete your essay.

You should try to write 300 words or more. Your essay will be graded on how well you use language, organize your essay, and develop your ideas.

Do you agree or disagree with the following statement?

Universities should only offer courses in their country's official language.

Use specific reasons to support your answer.

Practice Test 4

TEST DIRECTIONS

This test is designed to measure your ability to understand and to use English in an academic context. The test has four sections.

In the **Reading** section, you will read three passages and answer questions about them.

In the **Listening** section, you will listen to two dialogues and four talks and answer questions about them.

In the **Speaking** section, there are six tasks. The first two tasks ask you to speak based on your own personal experience. In the other four, you will read passages and/or listen to dialogues and talks, then speak based on what you have read and/or heard.

In the **Writing** section, there are two tasks. In the first task, you will read a passage, listen to a talk, then write based on what you have read and heard. The second task asks you to write based on your own personal experience and ideas.

There is a 10-minute break after the **Listening** section.

At the beginning of each section, there are directions that explain how to answer the questions or respond to the tasks in the section.

In the **Reading** and **Listening** sections, you should work carefully but quickly. You should try to answer every question to the best of your ability. Make an educated guess on questions that you are unsure of. In the **Speaking** and **Writing** sections, each task is separately timed. In each case, you should try to respond to the task as completely as possible in the given time.

READING SECTION

Directions: In this section of the test, you will read three passages. You will be tested on your ability to understand them by answering several questions on each passage.

While you read, you may take notes. You can then use your notes when answering questions.

Most questions are worth one point. Questions that are worth more than one point have a special note telling you how many total points they are worth.

You will have 60 minutes to read the three passages and answer all the questions. If you finish the questions before 60 minutes is up, you can go back and review your work in this section.

Passage 1

Hubble's "Tuning Fork" Galaxy Diagram

A In the 1920s, the American astronomer Edwin Hubble devised the first classification system for galaxies*. **B** Based on observations that he had made from the Mount Wilson Observatory in California, he created a classification system, identifying four galaxy "families": spiral, barred spiral, elliptical, and irregular. **C** Hubble then organized this classification system into a chart known as the "tuning fork" galaxy diagram. This diagram is still used today by astronomers to classify and compare newly discovered galaxies. **D**

Our solar system is a member of the Milky Way galaxy, which is thought to be a magnificently gigantic spiral galaxy. Such galaxies are easily identified by their beautiful spiral arms, which curve out from a bulging nucleus. Rich in gases and dust, spiral galaxies often give birth to new stars. On the Hubble tuning fork diagram, spiral galaxies are classified with the uppercase letter *S* (for *spiral*) followed by a lowercase *a*, *b*, or *c*. The letter represents the size and density of the galaxy, with *a* signifying the densest, largest galaxies and *c* the least dense, smallest galaxies.

Barred spiral galaxies are close cousins of spiral galaxies. The only real visible difference is a bar-shaped formation of stellar and interstellar material running directly through the galactic center. This bar has a strong gravitational pull that causes the galaxy to elongate across its center. Barred spiral galaxies are classified by the letters *SB* and the same lowercase letter system described previously. Recent discoveries have led to the theory that our Milky Way galaxy may actually be a barred spiral because of its elongated center.

An elliptical galaxy differs greatly from a spiral galaxy, even though—strangely—it is believed to be a product of an interaction between two spiral galaxies. When spiral galaxies collide or pass too close to each other, a great realignment occurs and an elliptical galaxy is formed. This kind of galaxy has no visible spiral arms and no surrounding disk, only a weak nucleus with no internal structure. It contains only a small amount of dust and gas and shows no evidence of star formation. Elliptical galaxies are classified by the capital letter *E*, followed by a number on a scale from zero to seven. The number pertains to the density and shape of the galaxy, with zero indicating the densest and most spherical galaxy and seven being the loosest and least formed.

Near the intersection of the three branches of Hubble's tuning fork galaxy diagram is a subgroup of galaxies—sometimes referred to as lenticular galaxies—that appear elliptical in form, but which have characteristics of spiral galaxies, most notably strong gravitational centers. For this reason, depending on whether they show spiral or barred spiral tendencies, lenticular galaxies are classified as either SO or SBO galaxies, respectively. They are clean visually, containing very little debris, but unlike elliptical galaxies, they have solid nuclei. An SBO galaxy has a bar-like formation stretching through the center that slightly elongates its shape. The visible difference is a lack of a halo or any surrounding debris. Lenticular galaxies are sometimes described as spiral galaxies without the arms.

Hubble's last category consists of the irregular galaxies, so named because of their asymmetrical and varied shapes. They are thought to be either the remnants of collisions between spiral galaxies, or very young galaxies that have not yet reached a symmetrical, rotating state. These galaxies are classified as Irr (for *irregular*), coupled with a Roman numeral I or II. Irr I galaxies look like misshapen spirals, and Irr II galaxies have very abstract shapes.

The Hubble Telescope, which was launched into space in 1990, was dedicated to discoveries made by Edwin Hubble and his contributions to world astronomy and science. It helps today's scientists observe and analyze galaxies that Hubble could only have dreamed of seeing. Until different shapes and sizes of galaxies are discovered, the tuning fork chart that Hubble created will continue to be used to identify and classify all of our future galactic discoveries.

galaxies: the large groups of stars and associated matter that the universe is made out of

1   According to the passage, Edwin Hubble made his galactic observations

   (A) through the Hubble Telescope.
   (B) from a California observatory.
   (C) using a tuning fork diagram.
   (D) with his own telescope.

2   Look at the four letters (**A**, **B**, **C**, and **D**) in the passage that show where the following sentence could be inserted.

   Resembling the shape of the tool musicians use to tune their instruments, the system consists of a stem (elliptical galaxies) and two branches (the two kinds of spiral galaxies).

   Where would the sentence best fit in the passage? Choose the letter for the square where this sentence should be added.

3   Which of the following sentences most closely expresses the important information in the highlighted sentence in the passage?

  (A) The many stars in spiral galaxies frequently produce gas and dust.

  (B) Due to the large amount of gases and dust in spiral galaxies, they often generate new stars.

  (C) In spite of the wealth of gas and dust in spiral galaxies, they seldom produce new stars.

  (D) Spiral galaxies are constantly engendering new stars, which are often dense with gases and particles.

4   The phrase close cousins of in paragraph 3 is closest in meaning to

  (A) descendents of.

  (B) intimately related to.

  (C) in relative proximity to.

  (D) situated next to.

5   What kind of galaxy would the tuning fork classification SBc represent?

  (A) a large elliptical galaxy

  (B) a dense spiral galaxy

  (C) a massive irregular galaxy

  (D) a small barred spiral galaxy

6   Astronomers today believe the Milky Way galaxy

  (A) is probably not a spiral galaxy.

  (B) is probably a barred spiral galaxy.

  (C) could be a barred spiral galaxy.

  (D) could be an elliptical galaxy.

7   The word debris in paragraph 5 is closest in meaning to

  (A) scattered material.

  (B) small galaxies.

  (C) asteroids.

  (D) energy.

8   According to the information in paragraph 5, lenticular galaxies resemble

  (A) elliptical galaxies.

  (B) barred spiral galaxies.

  (C) a subgroup of galaxies.

  (D) a halo.

9   It can be inferred from the passage that irregular galaxies

    (A) often end up disintegrating in huge explosions.

    (B) are the most common form of galaxies.

    (C) have several nuclei that create irregularity.

    (D) may sometimes form into spiral or elliptical galaxies.

10 The author discusses the Hubble Telescope in the last paragraph

    (A) to provide background about the telescope Hubble used for his research.

    (B) to introduce the idea that today's scientists may disprove Hubble's discoveries.

    (C) to suggest that Hubble had a very limited idea of the size of the universe.

    (D) to emphasize the importance of Hubble's contributions to astronomy.

11 According to the passage, Edwin Hubble contributed to astronomy mainly by

    (A) developing a classification system for galaxies.

    (B) devising a theory for the evolution of galaxies.

    (C) explaining the particle and gas structure of galaxies.

    (D) envisioning and planning the Hubble Telescope.

12 **Directions:** Find the phrases in the answer choices list that relate to spiral or elliptical galaxies. Write your answers in the appropriate place. TWO of the answer choices will NOT match either category. *This question is worth 4 points.*

Answer Choices	Spiral galaxies
A. Have arms that radiate out from a nucleus	
B. Contain little dust or gas	
C. Includes the "tuning fork" classification E7	**Elliptical galaxies**
D. Are similar to SB galaxies	
E. Have varied and asymetrical shapes	
F. Includes the Milky Way galaxy	
G. Are not believed to produce new stars	
H. Resemble lenticular galaxies	
I. Are usually relatively small	

Passage 2

Ellis Ruley, Folk artist

Like many artists, folk artist Ellis Ruley received virtually no recognition for his unique talent during his lifetime. He began to paint late in life, in an unreceptive and unnurturing environment. Nevertheless, he possessed a fiercely independent spirit and a highly creative impulse. Born on December 3, 1882 in Norwich, Connecticut, Ruley received little schooling and began working at a very early age. His family was one of only a handful of African American families in Norwich, none of which were prosperous. Ruley's family moved a total of 18 times in as many years from the time he was born, and both he and his father worked as laborers in coal yards and construction sites. His life proved unexceptional until the age of 42 when, while driving from work with a coworker one day, they were struck by a runaway truck, and Ruley ultimately received $25,000 in compensation for his injuries. This incident proved to be a pivotal event in Ruley's life, as the money enabled him to change his economic conditions overnight. He purchased three acres of land in a suburban area of Norwich, on which stood a small, antiquated house, bought a car, and married the divorced wife of his brother, a woman several years his junior named Wilhelmina. It was about this time, it is thought, that he first began to paint, although none of his work is actually dated.

Ruley had an intuitive sense of design and a strong sense of color. He seems to have started painting in order to decorate windows and wallpaper in his home, but he eventually switched his medium and for most of his career as an artist painted almost exclusively on posterboard, using ordinary house paints. Ruley's paintings were deeply connected to nature, a fact not only noticeable in his work but one that was reflected in his daily life. He called himself a "naturalist" and tried to be as self-sufficient as possible, growing vegetables and fruit trees on his land. He made a pond so that animals could come and drink from it and swim. **A** These backyard scenes from nature were reproduced by Ruley throughout his work, metamorphosing on his ubiquitous posterboard into jungles and forests. **B** He painted birds and flowers and animals, waterfalls, his own versions of hunters and hula dancers and pop stars and famous Americans. **C** He painted horses, canoes, zebras, farmhouses and Adam and Eve—but with a unique style that created a strangely unsettling, dreamlike effect. **D** Ruley was painting his own visions of paradise, but there was almost always a sense of danger or foreboding even in the most bucolic scenes.

Ruley's paintings have been compared to those of 19th-century French painter Henri Rousseau or 20th-century Haitian artist Philomé Obin, but Ruley's work falls into the category of folk art inspired in part by African folklore. In African myth, animals are spirits, with the ability to change form and help people escape bondage. Hence much of Ruley's work fits into a tradition of African American artists identifying spirits in nature. In Ruley's painting *Waterfall*, ghostly mask-like forms seem to beckon from the water. In *See How Pretty*, running water forms skull-like shapes, representing spirits in the water, as two skeletal young girls approach a stream. *Waterfall* and *See How Pretty* are representative of the fact that in African cultures, works of art have often been used as a means of channeling the forces of spirits and nature and protecting oneself from them.

At the age of 77, Ruley died as the result of mysterious wounds to his head. A racist extremist group was suspected although the culprits were never identified. At the time of his death, many of his own neighbors did not even know he was an artist. The only exhibition of his work during his lifetime was on December 2, 1952, at a show at the Norwich Art School, which received a brief, though positive, review in the *Norwich Bulletin-Record*. In spite of its lack of visibility during Ruley's lifetime, his primitive work possesses, as that review of his show pointed out, a "directness of approach, sincerity and a love for his work," that many still appreciate today. Joseph Gualtieri, curator of the Slater Museum, and producer of Ruley's one show, later remarked, "He was a painter of the exotic . . . he brings to his work a freshness of vision, full of stimulating surprises and unexpected happenings."

13 Based on information in paragraph 1, it can be inferred that

   (A) during Ruley's childhood, there were many African American families in Norwich.

   (B) Ruley displayed artistic creativity while still a child, but developed it only later.

   (C) Ruley's work received considerable recognition after his death.

   (D) after the age of 42, Ruley was no longer able to perform manual labor.

14 The phrase pivotal event in the passage is closest in meaning to

   (A) turning point.

   (B) surprising outcome.

   (C) hopeful circumstance.

   (D) likely prospect.

15 According to the passage, all of the following are true of Ellis Ruley EXCEPT

   (A) he married a woman who was younger than himself.

   (B) he divorced his first wife to marry Wilhelmina.

   (C) he moved house after his accident.

   (D) he and his father held similar jobs.

16 Look at the four letters (**A**, **B**, **C**, and **D**) in the passage that show where the following sentence could be inserted into the passage.

This gave him an opportunity to observe them close up.

Where would the sentence best fit in the passage? Choose the letter for the square where this sentence should be added.

17 According to the passage, why did Ruley refer to himself as a naturalist?

  (A) He often included themes from nature in his work.

  (B) He preferred to use paint that was made from natural materials.

  (C) He painted primarily out-of-doors.

  (D) He believed that consuming natural foods improved his work.

18 Which of the following best explains the word folk in the passage?

  (A) having to do with ordinary people

  (B) having to do with professional artists

  (C) having to do with undiscovered talent

  (D) having to do with standard techniques

19 The author describes Ruley's art by

  (A) explaining how it was affected by his medium.

  (B) showing how it became more and more sophisticated over time.

  (C) arguing that his work is superior to that of more famous folk artists.

  (D) identifying the influence of myth on his painting.

20 Which of the following sentences most closely expresses the important information in the highlighted sentence in the passage?

  (A) Ruley's work, though not well known while he was alive, is now admired for qualities that were originally pointed out in a newspaper article about his show.

  (B) Despite the primitiveness of Ruley's work, one newspaper reviewer who attended his show particularly appreciated his artistic talent and unique vision.

  (C) According to one newspaper reviewer who attended his show, Ruley's work, which was not appreciated for many years, would have been better received had it demonstrated more directness and honesty.

  (D) Even though the people of Ruley's day felt that his work lacked vision, one newspaper reviewer who attended his show pointed out some of its remarkable characteristics.

21 The word curator in the passage is closest in meaning to

  (A) director.

  (B) founder.

  (C) teacher.

  (D) neighbor.

22 It can be inferred from the passage that

(A) Ruley's first show received both favorable and unfavorable reviews.

(B) Ruley's neighbors had little interest in art and culture.

(C) Ruley's talent was appreciated by the leaders of the Norwich Art School.

(D) Ruley died before he could fully develop his artistic vision.

23 **Directions:** Below is an introductory sentence for a short summary of the passage. Complete the summary by choosing the THREE answer choices that express key ideas in the passage. Sentences that express ideas that are NOT in the passage or mention minor details do NOT belong in the summary. *This question is worth 2 points.*

Ellis Ruley was a folk artist with a primitive yet compelling style.

Answer Choices	
A. The first half of his life was not easy one, but a midlife change in his circumstances made it possible for him to discover and develop his artistic talent.	D. Ruley included a wide variety of everyday subjects in his paintings, treating them in a way that gave the viewer a sense of peace and safety.
B. Ruley was probably killed by a group of extremists who resented the attention his work had gained.	E. Ruley based much of his work on themes derived from African folklore.
C. Ruley started life as a laborer, but spent his last few decades living as a farmer while painting in his spare time.	F. Ruley only had one exhibition of his work in his lifetime that received a positive review, and died before many even knew he was an artist.

Passage 3

Nuclear Reactors

Nuclear reactors, when first developed, were hailed as virtually unlimited sources of cheap, clean, and efficiently produced energy. However, in the last 50 years, the public perception of nuclear reactors has changed from acceptance and hope to fear and distrust. This is due variously to the association of nuclear energy with nuclear weapons, to the work of outspoken environmental critics, and to two relatively recent major accidents at commercial nuclear reactors.

The design of a nuclear power plant is similar to that of a conventional power plant that burns fossil fuel. The difference is that instead of providing heat by using a burner, a nuclear power plant generates heat by means of a nuclear reaction. In both instances, a cooling fluid such as water carries the heat to a steam generator. The steam then drives a turbine connected to an electrical generator. The advantage of nuclear reactors is that they generate electricity without burning coal or oil. This avoids air pollution.

Nuclear fission produces the energy generated by nuclear reactors. Fission is the splitting apart of a large atom into smaller atoms, and it causes the simultaneous generation of heat and neutrons. The "fuel" of a nuclear reactor is a fissionable material, such as uranium-235, which undergoes fission when struck by a slow-moving neutron. On average, fission of uranium-235 produces 2.4 neutrons. The two neutrons can cause two fissions. The four neutrons released can produce four fissions, and so forth. The number of fissions and the energy released quickly escalate. Reactions that multiply in this fashion are called chain reactions, and they generate large amounts of heat.

In a nuclear reactor, UO_2 pellets—uranium enriched to about 3 percent uranium-235—are encased in tubes made of   either zirconium or stainless steel alloy, thus forming fuel rods. The radioactive fission products remain bound inside the pellets. The entire assembly is confined within a large steel pressure vessel with thick walls, which in turn is enclosed in a robust concrete containment structure. A commercial-type power reactor simply can never explode like a nuclear bomb because the uranium-235 concentration is too low. However, if the nuclear core overheats, there may be sufficient damage to release radioactive materials into the environment.

A more vexing problem posed by nuclear power is the disposal of radioactive wastes produced by the reactor. Highly radioactive fission products accumulate in the fuel rods as the reactor operates. Originally, engineers envisioned keeping fuel rods in pools for several months at the reactor site to allow decay of short-lived radioactive nuclei. The rods would then be transported in shielded containers to reprocessing plants, where the fuel would be separated from the fission products. However, reprocessing plants have been plagued by operational difficulties, and there is intense opposition to the transport of nuclear wastes on highways in the United States. At present, spent fuel rods are stored at reactor sites. However, storage poses a major problem because the fission products are extremely radioactive. Approximately 20 half-lives are required for their radioactivity to reach levels acceptable for biological exposure. Based on the 28.8-year half-life of strontium-90—one of the shorter-lived and most dangerous of the products—nuclear wastes must be stored for 600 years. A considerable amount of research has been devoted to finding better ways to dispose of radioactive wastes. One possibility is to form a glass, ceramic, or synthetic rock from the wastes, thus immobilizing them. These solid materials, placed in containers of high corrosion-resistance and durability, could be buried deep underground.

Nuclear power plants have numerous safety features. Nevertheless, there have been two major accidents in the history of civil nuclear-power generation. One of them occurred in the United States in 1979 at the Three Mile Island plant in Pennsylvania. This accident severely damaged the reactor. The containment building that housed the reactor prevented significant release of radioactivity despite the fact that about half of the reactor melted. **A** The accident was caused by mechanical failure and operator confusion. **B** The radiation was contained, and there were no adverse health or environmental consequences. **C** In 1986, explosions at the

Chernobyl plant in the former USSR resulted in 31 immediate deaths and radioactive fallout that has dramatically raised the cancer and birth defects rate in areas close to the plant and in European countries downwind from the disaster. **D**

24 The author discusses fission in paragraph 3 in order to

    (A) describe the process whereby reactors generate high temperatures.

    (B) show why nuclear power is potentially dangerous to the environment.

    (C) explain the meaning of the terms *fissionable material* and *chain reaction.*

    (D) provide a detailed explanation of how chemicals are converted to heat.

25 The word robust in paragraph 4 is closest in meaning to

    (A) flavorful.

    (B) healthy.

    (C) determined.

    (D) sturdy.

26 According to the passage, storing spent fuel rods at nuclear reactor sites is a problem because of

    (A) the time required for the rods' radioactivity to reach safe levels.

    (B) the dangers in transporting the rods long distances via highways.

    (C) the operational complications at reprocessing plants.

    (D) the reactor sites' vulnerability to spontaneous explosion.

27 The purpose of converting nuclear waste into rock and burying it would be to

    (A) prevent it from being transported on highways.

    (B) accelerate the radioactive decay process.

    (C) keep it from leaking into the environment.

    (D) minimize the risk of a nuclear explosion.

28 Based on information in paragraph 3, which of the following best explains the term fission?

Based on information in paragraph 5, which of the following best explains the term vexing?

    (A) worrying

    (B) irritating

    (C) appeasing

    (D) short lived

29 According to the passage, the damage caused by the Three Mile Island accident was limited by

   Ⓐ the burial of spent fuel rods deep underground.

   Ⓑ built-in mechanical backup systems.

   Ⓒ the quick reaction of operators and supervisors.

   Ⓓ the structure that contained the reactor.

30 Look at the four letters (**A**, **B**, **C**, and **D**) in the passage that show where the following sentence could be inserted.

The same cannot be said about the other recent major accident at a nuclear power plant.

Where would the sentence best fit in the passage? Choose the letter for the square where this sentence should be added.

31 Which of the following is NOT mentioned in the passage as a potential problem associated with nuclear power?

   Ⓐ leaks of radioactivity into the environment

   Ⓑ a huge nuclear explosion

   Ⓒ the storage of waste materials

   Ⓓ mechanical failure

32 Which of the following most accurately reflects the author's opinion about nuclear power?

   Ⓐ Whatever benefits it may have, nuclear power is far too dangerous to be used as an energy source today.

   Ⓑ While scientists must address the serious risks associated with it, nuclear power remains a viable and efficient option for producing energy.

   Ⓒ Nuclear power is society's best hope for a clean, long-term energy source; people's fears of nuclear power are based largely on paranoia.

   Ⓓ There are valid concerns about the safety of nuclear power, but science has already resolved most of the problems associated with the technology.

33 According to the passage, all of the following are advantages of nuclear power EXCEPT

   Ⓐ it produces little air pollution.

   Ⓑ its fuel source is cheap and plentiful.

   Ⓒ its waste products are easily disposed of.

   Ⓓ it produces electricity more efficiently than fossil fuels.

34 Directions: Below is an introductory sentence for a short summary of the passage. Complete the summary by choosing the THREE answer choices that express key ideas in the passage. Sentences that express ideas that are NOT in the passage or mention minor details do NOT belong in the summary. *This question is worth 2 points.*

Once hailed as a clean and plentiful energy source, nuclear power has fallen out of favor largely on account of concerns over its safety.

Answer Choices	
A. One of the most serious challenges nuclear power poses is the disposable waste materials, some of which remain radioactive for centuries.	D. Enriched uranium pellets are formed into fuel rods, which are housed within a steel vessel, and this in turn is incased in a thick cement structure.
B. Some scientists have proposed forming nuclear waste into synthetic rock, a more stable state in which to store material.	E. Some nuclear waste materials take more than 600 years to decay to safe levels.
C. Nuclear reactors produce energy through fission, which triggers a series of chain reactions, releasing large amounts of heat.	F. Although they have been relatively few in number, accidents like those ate Three Mile Island and Chernobyl have shaken the public's confidence in nuclear power.

LISTENING SECTION

Directions: In this section of the test, you will hear dialogues and academic talks, and you will be tested on your ability to understand them. You will hear each dialogue and academic talk only once, and then answer some questions after each is finished. The questions ask about the main idea, supporting details, and the way the speakers use language. Answer each question based on what is stated or implied by the speakers. You cannot go back to a question once you have answered it. Answer every question in the order that it appears.

While you listen, you may take notes. You can then use your notes when answering questions.

You will see the following headphones icon next to some questions: This icon indicates that you will hear part of the dialogue or academic talk repeated for the question.

Most questions are worth one point. Questions that are worth more than one point have a special note telling you how many total points they are worth.

You will be given 20 minutes to answer all the questions in this section. This does not include the time to listen to the dialogues and academic talks.

Dialogue 1

🎧 **Track 40**

Directions: Now use your notes to help you answer the questions.

1 What is the focus of the professor's class project?

    Ⓐ ways to teach a five-part lesson

    Ⓑ how to teach a grammar lesson

    Ⓒ the experience of student teaching

    Ⓓ the demographics of a particular school

2 Why did the student need to talk with the professor?

    Ⓐ to get an extension on his project

    Ⓑ to clarify the parts of the project

    Ⓒ to explain why he was so late

    Ⓓ to turn in the first part of the project

3 What subject does the student teach?

    Ⓐ Math

    Ⓑ Spanish

    Ⓒ Physical education

    Ⓓ European history

4 Listen to part of the dialogue again, and then answer the question. What is the professor implying?

    Ⓐ It is not always obvious that a student is in class.

    Ⓑ She has trouble remembering all of the students' names.

    Ⓒ She has caught the student sleeping in class.

    Ⓓ It is difficult to answer all the students' questions in a large class.

5 Listen to part of the dialogue again, and then answer the question. What can be inferred about the student?

    Ⓐ He is going to quit his job.

    Ⓑ He is upset about missing class.

    Ⓒ He does not like to drive when it rains.

    Ⓓ He was having a difficult day.

Dialogue 2

🎧 **Track 41**

Directions: Now use your notes to help you answer the questions.

6 Why does the student go to the administrative office?

    Ⓐ to pay her student fees

    Ⓑ to resolve a problem

    Ⓒ to register for a class

    Ⓓ to translate wire instructions

7 What has happened with the bank transfer?

    Ⓐ An overpayment was made.

    Ⓑ It was not received by the school.

    Ⓒ It was sent to the correct account.

    Ⓓ It was returned to the sender.

8 Listen to part of the dialogue again, and then answer the question. What does the administrator mean when he says this: 🎧

    Ⓐ He is asking if the student understands the policy.

    Ⓑ He is telling the student not to go to Monday classes.

    Ⓒ He is asking the student to pay the school fees.

    Ⓓ He wants the student to come back on Monday.

9 What does the administrator offer to do?

(A) extend the payment deadline

(B) refund the incorrect payment

(C) set up a meeting with his manager

(D) send the student a copy of the receipt

10 What will the administrator probably do?

(A) ask the student to speak to the manager in person

(B) report his decision to his manager

(C) place an immediate call to his manager

(D) ask his manager to confirm his decision

Academic Talk 1: Film Studies

🎧 **Track 42**

Directions: Now use your notes to help you answer the questions.

11 What is the talk mainly about?

(A) the evolution of comedy films

(B) a comparison between two comedians

(C) a contrast between silent and sound films

(D) an examination of one comedian's work

12 What does the professor say is interesting about Keaton?

Choose 2 answers.

A He never showed a smile in his films.

B He made more films than any other comedian.

C He used his hat for comic effect.

D He was the only comedian who directed his own films.

13 What can be inferred about Keaton's approach to filmmaking?

(A) He inserted many social observations in his comedy.

(B) He eliminated physical activity in favor of intellectual humor.

(C) He blended the slapstick with the philosophical.

(D) He preferred to act and work the camera instead of direct.

14 Listen to part of the talk again, and then answer the question. Why does the professor say this: 🎧

    Ⓐ to suggest that the student is getting ahead of the professor

    Ⓑ to encourage other students to join in the discussion

    Ⓒ to express uncertainty about moving on to a new topic too quickly

    Ⓓ to clarify that she has finished discussing the previous topic

15 Listen to part of the talk again, and then answer the question. What does the professor mean when she says: 🎧

    Ⓐ The comedian liked using food props in his comedy films.

    Ⓑ The comedian would use everything at his disposal for good effect.

    Ⓒ The comedian sometimes put some weak scenes in his comedy.

    Ⓓ The comedian included too much in the film and ruined the humor.

16 According to the talk, which of the following are events from Buster Keaton's life that helped shape his career?

Choose 3 answers.

    Ⓐ meeting Roscoe Arbuckle

    Ⓑ moving to New York

    Ⓒ joining a vaudeville group when he was 17 years old

    Ⓓ working in the film *The Butcher Boy*

    Ⓔ starring in several movies that Charlie Chaplin directed

Academic Talk 2: Biology

🎧 **Track 43**

Directions: Now use your notes to help you answer the questions.

17 What is the discussion mainly about?

    Ⓐ what diabetes is

    Ⓑ how diabetes causes disease

    Ⓒ what diabetics should do

    Ⓓ how to prevent diabetes from occurring

18 Which of the following facts about diabetes does the professor mention?

    Ⓐ it is common in overweight people

    Ⓑ many diabetics are never diagnosed

    Ⓒ it can cause problems like kidney failure and heart disease

    Ⓓ six percent of the U.S. population has diabetes

19 Listen to part of the talk again, and then answer the question. What does the student suggest?

(A) People with diabetes are unfortunate.

(B) There are no known cures for diabetes.

(C) Reducing sugar intake can cure diabetes.

(D) Diabetes cannot be cured if left untreated.

20 Listen to part of the talk again, and then answer the question. What does the professor mean when he says this: 🎧

(A) Diabetics should eliminate sweets from their diets.

(B) Diabetics actually need to eat more sweets than the average person.

(C) Diabetics and nondiabetics who want to eat sweets should check with their doctors first.

(D) Diabetics and nondiabetics can eat sweets if they want to.

21 Listen to part of the talk again, and then answer the question. What is the purpose of the professor's comment?

(A) to emphasize the danger of diabetes

(B) to describe a focus of scientific research

(C) to demonstrate how diabetes can be managed

(D) to illustrate his concern for people with diabetes

22 Which of the following are diabetics required to do regularly?

(A) Consume foods that are high in sugar.

(B) Consume excess fats and starches.

(C) Donate blood on a weekly basis.

(D) Measure the amount of glucose in their blood.

Academic Talk 3: Film Studies

🎧 **Track 44**

Directions: Now use your notes to help you answer the questions.

23 What is the talk mainly about?

(A) adapting a book into a film

(B) a novelist who became a screenwriter

(C) why books are better than movies

(D) a book that was made into an unpopular movie

24 Why does the professor mention the first scene in the film, *Bonfire of the Vanities*?

    (A) It replicates the opening episode in the book exactly.

    (B) It shows the director's careful selection of character.

    (C) It shows a very different perspective from the book's.

    (D) It is the only scene that is effective in both book and film.

25 According to the talk, what can be inferred about film adaptations?

    (A) They are often better than the original books.

    (B) They are often inferior to the original books.

    (C) They are usually just as good as the original books.

    (D) They are sometimes written by the books' authors.

26 Listen to part of the talk again, and then answer the question. Why does the professor say this: 🎧

    (A) to let the students know it is time to be quiet

    (B) to help introduce the day's subject

    (C) to find out how many people know the expression

    (D) to give the students some time to think

27 Listen to part of the talk again, and then answer the question. What does the student mean by this: 🎧

    (A) Movies adapted from books rarely make a profit.

    (B) A movie is usually shorter than the book from which it was adapted.

    (C) Movies adapted from books cannot really compare to the original.

    (D) A movie is really just a short version of the original book.

28 In the talk, the professor describes a number of things that can be affected by an adaptation. Choose 3 of the answer choices below that were mentioned in the talk.

	Yes	No
A. Number of characters		
B. Works of art		
C. Politics		
D. Details in the book		
E. Dialogue		

Academic Talk 4: Astronomy

 Track 45

Directions: Now use your notes to help you answer the questions.

29　What is the main topic of this talk?

　　Ⓐ　two space probes sponsored by the European Space Agency

　　Ⓑ　how space probes may resolve mysteries about Mercury

　　Ⓒ　similarities between the planet Mercury and the moon

　　Ⓓ　Einstein's predictions about Mercury's eliptical orbit

30　Why does the professor begin by discussing how difficult it is to see Mercury from Earth?

　　Ⓐ　to remind students of the main idea of the previous talk

　　Ⓑ　to suggest that Mercury is too close to the sun to explore

　　Ⓒ　to explain why students may be unfamiliar with Mercury

　　Ⓓ　to emphasize how little we know about Mercury

31　What can be inferred about Mercury?

　　Ⓐ　A space probe has never been put in orbit around the planet.

　　Ⓑ　It has a dense atmosphere because it orbits so close to the sun.

　　Ⓒ　It has held little interest for scientists since the mid-1970s.

　　Ⓓ　It is the most mysterious planet in the solar system.

32　Why are the *Mariner 10* pictures all of one side of Mercury?

　　Ⓐ　The camera broke down halfway through the mission due to extreme heat.

　　Ⓑ　The probe left Mercury before the planet had turned to reveal the other side.

　　Ⓒ　The sun's rays were too bright to allow pictures to be taken of the other side.

　　Ⓓ　The probe's camera focused on the side of Mercury not visible from Earth.

33　What will spectrometry determine about Mercury?

　　Ⓐ　whether Einstein's general theory of relativity explains its orbit

　　Ⓑ　whether the volcanoes on the far side of the planet are active

　　Ⓒ　the reasons for the planet's unusually strong magnetic field

　　Ⓓ　the reasons for the planet's present size and composition

34 What is true of Mercury's magnetic field?

(A) It is similar to those of the other inner planets.

(B) It will present danger to the BepiColombo probe.

(C) It exists because the planet is so close to the sun.

(D) It cannot work in the same way as that of Earth.

SPEAKING SECTION

Directions: In this section, you will be asked to respond to a variety of tasks and topics. There are six tasks. Respond to each task as completely as you can, always speaking clearly.

For tasks 1 and 2, you will speak about topics that are familiar to you. Your responses will be graded on your ability to speak about the topics clearly.

For tasks 3 and 4, you will be asked to read a short text. For each task, you will be asked a question about what you have read and heard. You will need to use information from the text and the talk to answer the questions. Your responses will be graded on your ability to speak clearly and accurately about what you have read and heard.

For tasks 5 and 6, you will hear part of a dialogue or an academic talk. For each task, you will then answer a question about what you have heard. Your responses will be graded on your ability to speak clearly and accurately about what you have heard.

You are allowed to take notes during the reading and listening. You are allowed to use your notes to help you respond. Read the directions for each task closely.

For each task, you will be given a short time to prepare your response. You will be given a certain amount of time to speak. Use a watch or clock to time yourself.

Task 1

Directions: Task One. For this task, you will be asked to speak about a topic that is familiar to you. You will hear a question. You will then have 15 seconds to prepare your response and 45 seconds to speak.

 Track 46

Describe a movie you've recently watched and explain why you liked it. Include details and examples to support your explanation.

> 15 seconds to prepare
> 45 seconds to speak

Task 2

Directions: Task Two. For this task, you will give your opinion about a topic that is familiar to you. You will hear a question. You will then have 15 seconds to prepare your response and 45 seconds to speak.

 Track 47

Some people think that television, the Internet, and other electronic media make the printed book obsolete as a source of information or entertainment. Other people say that printed books will continue to play an important role in society. Which view do you agree with? Include details and examples in your explanation.

> 15 seconds to prepare
> 45 seconds to speak

Task 3

Directions: Task Three. For this task, you will read a short text and then listen to a dialogue about the same topic. You will hear a question about what you have read and heard. You will then have 30 seconds to prepare your response and 60 seconds to speak.

South Shore University's Business School Club is looking for a person to be its coordinator in the upcoming academic year. You will have 45 seconds to read the announcement. Begin reading now.

Get Involved!

Are you a senior in the School of Business? Are you looking for a way to make a contribution to your school in your last year? Are you interested in making great contacts with business owners in the local community? The South Shore University Business School Club seeks a dynamic graduating senior with great organizational skills to be its coordinator for the coming academic year. The coordinator has overall responsibility for planning and implementing all club activities for the year. For more information about this exciting position, please refer to the Student Services website.

Track 48

The man tries to persuade the woman to do something. Say what he tries to persuade her to do and explain the reasons he gives.

> 30 seconds to prepare
> 60 seconds to speak

Task 4

Directions: Task Four. For this task, you will read a short text and then hear a talk about the same topic. You will hear a question about what you have read and heard. After you hear the question, you will then have 30 seconds to prepare your response and 60 seconds to speak.

Now read the passage about computer hacking. You have 45 seconds to read the passage. Begin reading now.

Hacking: Crime or Service to Society?

There exist two divergent views on hacking. The definition of the term itself shows that divergence; a standard dictionary will tell you that two of the term's meanings are: a) to create computer programs for fun, and b) to gain illegal access to a computer.

So which is it? Are hackers simply people with inquisitive minds who wish to probe the limits of computer systems—and thereby showing where things can be improved? Or are they devious criminals who have taken simple crude vandalism to a higher—and much farther reaching—level? The answer to that question, like so many others, probably depends on who you speak to. Those with a knack for computers and a rebellious spirit will probably tell you that hacking is all in good fun. But those on the other side of that "fun"—people who have had their finances scrambled or personal information released to the world, will probably take offense at such a description of the act of hacking.

 Track 49

Two opinions on computer hacking are given in the reading. Explain which of these views the professor holds and how she supports her opinion.

> 30 seconds to prepare
> 60 seconds to speak

Task 5

Directions: Task Five. For this task, you will listen to a dialogue. You will hear a question about it. You will then have 20 seconds to prepare your response and 60 seconds to speak.

 Track 50

The students discuss two possible solutions to the man's problem. Describe the problem. Then state which solution you prefer and explain why.

> 20 seconds to prepare
> 60 seconds to speak

Task 6

Directions: Task Six. For this task, you will hear a short academic talk. You will hear a question about it. You will then have 20 seconds to prepare your response and 60 seconds to speak.

Track 51

Using points and examples from the talk, explain the factors that contributed to the loss of Holland's colony of New Amsterdam.

> 20 seconds to prepare
> 60 seconds to speak

WRITING SECTION

Directions: You will need to listen to Track 52 for this section.

This section is designed to measure your ability to write in English. There are two tasks.

For the first task, you will read a short text and listen to an academic talk. You will answer a question about what you have read and heard. For the second task, you will use your knowledge and experience to answer a question.

Task 1

Directions: For this task, you will have 3 minutes to read a short text. You may take notes if you wish. Then you will hear an academic talk on the same topic. You may take notes while you listen.

You will then read a question that asks about the relationship between the text and the talk. You will have 20 minutes to write a response. Using information from the text and talk, answer the question as completely as you can. You will not be asked to give your opinion. You will be able to review the text while you write. You may use your notes to help you write your response.

You should try to write 150 words or more. Your response will be graded on the quality, completeness, and accuracy of your writing. If you finish early, you may move on to the second task.

In this question, you will read a short passage and then listen to a talk on the same topic. You will then have 20 minutes to write an answer to the question that follows, using your notes and the written passage for reference.

You now have 3 minutes to read the passage. After you read the passage, listen to the talk.

Many American companies have decided to outsource jobs performed by Americans to workers in other countries. This issue has fast become controversial, as some advocates of outsourcing see it as the only way to keep their companies competitive. Opponents of outsourcing view it as the number-one reason for unemployment in the United States. Who's right?

Multinational companies first began to outsource as a way to gain visibility in foreign markets where American workers were unfamiliar with the local business customs. As time passed, the combination of skilled workers and low wages led American companies to support the infrastructure in these countries with an eye to eventually moving nonessential operations to these locations.

In reality, this shift of such operations as telemarketing and customer service closely parallels a shift that occurred 25 to 30 years ago when U.S. companies moved these same operations to rural areas where labor costs were more favorable. That sort of domestic outsourcing also raised eyebrows at the time, but many people today feel that it's completely acceptable for a company's headquarters to be located in New York City, while the lower-wage positions are located in smaller cities where the cost of labor and operating budgets are much lower. This is simply good business sense—keeping costs low and production high—that makes products and services more affordable.

Those who view outsourcing as responsible for the loss of U.S. jobs are terribly misguided. Outsourcing is a valid business proposition that has the best interests of the U.S. public in mind. By sending operations offshore, American companies are securing their own financial future and that of the American public—not causing rampant unemployment.

 Track 52

Summarize the points made in the lecture you just heard, and then compare the speaker's opinion with the opinion stated in the reading.

Task 2

Directions: For this task, you will be asked to write an essay in which you state, explain, and support your opinion on an issue. You will have 30 minutes to complete your essay.

You should try to write 300 words or more. Your essay will be graded on how well you use language, organize your essay, and develop your ideas.

> Some parents educate their children at home rather than in public schools because they believe that they can provide a better education themselves.

Do you agree that homeschooling offers advantages over public education? Use specific reasons and examples to support your answer.

Listening
Scripts

PRACTICE TEST 1

LISTENING SECTION

Dialogue 1

Track 1

NARRATOR:	Listen to a dialogue between a professor and a student.
STUDENT:	Professor Smith! I was planning to drop by your office later on today, to, uh, to discuss my midterm. Will you, ah, have a few minutes for me a little bit later?
PROFESSOR:	Actually, the 401 midterm is tomorrow, so I have several appointments this afternoon—but if you have a few minutes now, I'd be more than happy to discuss the midterm with you right here.
STUDENT:	I don't have class until two-fifteen, but I wouldn't want to interrupt your lunch …
PROFESSOR:	No, it's no problem. Please, take a seat. So, what's up?
STUDENT:	I wanted to talk to you about my midterm … I didn't do as well as I expected to. I studied but I just blanked on the second part. Is there anything I can do for extra credit to boost my grade a little bit?
PROFESSOR:	You know, I was wondering what happened to you.
STUDENT:	I just completely blanked on it. I knew it so well the night before, but I just lost it all during the test. I really do understand it, I'm, I'm not sure what happened …
PROFESSOR:	I really don't believe in extra credit projects, because they're usually done at home. It's not fair to the other students who've had to answer questions under pressure in class, and with time limits, too. But what did you have in mind?
STUDENT:	Oh. I hadn't really thought about it … maybe I could retake the part of the test I messed up on? Or write a paper?
PROFESSOR:	To be honest, I think you'd need to do something a little, uh, more involved than either of those. You'd really need to put some thought into a project and come up with something that demonstrates that you understand the concept, but also show that you can take it a step further than what we did in class and what was tested on the exam. I suppose, if you're able to do that, I could consider giving you some extra credit for it.
STUDENT:	Great! Thanks so much!
PROFESSOR:	I'm not guaranteeing that I'll accept your project, though. It has to be something really extraordinary to qualify for extra credit. Remember, it has to be more in-depth than what we've covered in class. I want this project to be a, um, a learning experience for you, so it should also synthesize some material that we haven't yet covered in class, not just reiterate what we've already discussed.

STUDENT:	Okay … Maybe I can do an analysis of the more involved structures that the book doesn't cover? I can do some extra research …
PROFESSOR:	Sure, something like that might work. Wow, is it five to two already? I have to run to class. Why don't you email me your proposal for the project, and I'll get back to you to let you know if it will work.
STUDENT:	Great! Thanks so much. I'll have a proposal to you by tomorrow morning.
NARRATOR:	Now use your notes to help you answer the questions.
	Why does the student meet with the professor?
	Does the professor normally accept extra credit projects?
	Listen to part of the dialogue again, and then answer the question.
PROFESSOR:	You know, I was wondering what happened to you.
NARRATOR:	Why does the professor say this?
	What will the student do for extra credit?
	What will the student probably do that afternoon?

Dialogue 2

Track 2

NARRATOR:	Listen to a dialogue between a student and a professor.
PROFESSOR:	Please come in, Molly. I'm sorry to keep you waiting.
STUDENT:	No problem, Professor Warren. Thanks for seeing me.
PROFESSOR:	Uh, you said on the phone that you wanted to speak with me about majoring in women's studies.
STUDENT:	Yes, um … actually, I'll be double-majoring.
PROFESSOR:	Oh? In … ?
STUDENT:	Sociology as well as women's studies.
PROFESSOR:	That's a good combination since sociology offers lots of courses that are cross-disciplinary with WS, like uh … let me get the catalogue here.
STUDENT:	Like Sociology of Women?
PROFESSOR:	That's right … here's the catalogue.
STUDENT:	I'm taking Sociology of Women now with Professor Davis.
PROFESSOR:	Mmm, that would serve as an elective for both WS and sociology.
STUDENT:	Sort of like the "two birds with one stone" thing, right?
PROFESSOR:	Uh, you could say that. Are you familiar with the requirements?
STUDENT:	No. I mean, I must have seen them in the catalogue when I registered, but that was a couple of months ago.
PROFESSOR:	Well, basically, you'll need to take the introductory course, followed by Feminist Theories, and Women's History—those are required, plus five electives.
STUDENT:	That could be from any department?

PROFESSOR:	Oh, any department that's cross-referenced with WS—meaning that the course will fulfill an elective requirement in both departments.
STUDENT:	That seems easy enough. I could finish the coursework in less than a year, going full-time.
PROFESSOR:	But we have other requirements for the major, besides the courses.
STUDENT:	Oh? I uh, I don't remember reading about that.
PROFESSOR:	I'm sure it's in the book. Let's see, uh, yes. You'll need to complete an internship at a women's organization.
STUDENT:	You mean like the, the National Organization for Women?
PROFESSOR:	No—well, I suppose, if you found an opportunity to intern there, or rather at your local chapter, of course you could do that. But we'd prefer something more community-oriented, like a women's shelter or a women's health clinic.
STUDENT:	Would this be volunteer or paid?
PROFESSOR:	Oh, no, no pay here. This is purely for the experience, about three hours a week, of helping a small nonprofit organization that focuses on important women's issues. Then you'd come back to the school each week and report on your experience to your classmates in the Women's Seminar.
STUDENT:	It sounds like, like a lot of work, but I think it's a wonderful thing to do. I may even make connections there for a future job.
PROFESSOR:	It's quite possible. Some of our students who've interned at some of these places have actually gone back to work there.
NARRATOR:	Now use your notes to help you answer the questions.
	What is the professor referring to when he says WS?
	What else is required in addition to the coursework?
	What can be inferred about cross-disciplinary courses?
	Listen to part of the dialogue again, and then answer the question.
PROFESSOR:	Uh, you could say that. Are you familiar with the requirements?
STUDENT:	No. I mean, I must have seen them in the catalogue when I registered, but that was a couple of months ago.
NARRATOR:	What does the student's answer mean?
	Why is the student looking forward to joining a women's organization?

Academic Talk 1: Art History

Track 3

NARRATOR:	Listen to part of a talk in an art history class.
PROFESSOR:	Okay, let's get started. Today, we're going to continue our discussion by talking about public art. Who can sum up the text-book's definition of public art for the class?
STUDENT A:	I think the book says that it's, ah, it's basically any work of art that's readily available to the general population—it's either mounted in an outdoor space, or in a building that's accessible to the public.

PROFESSOR: So by that definition, wouldn't an exhibit at a museum be public art, because the building is somewhat open to the public? Or is there more to it than that?

STUDENT A: No ... it doesn't really apply to art that can be found in muse-ums or galleries. It's more like art that uses the public space as part of the exhibit. One of the examples in the book was Michelangelo's painting on the ceiling of the Sistine Chapel. I guess it sort of applies to buildings where you wouldn't expect to see art ... like in churches, or Keith Haring's graffiti in New York City's subways ...

PROFESSOR: That's it. You hit it right on the head. The distinction between public art and most other forms of art is that public art turns up in places where it's least expected—painted church ceilings, statues in parks, subway graffiti ...

Does anyone remember the Cow Parade exhibit we had in the city a few summers ago? I see some of you shaking your heads. Well, during Cow Parade, there were about 250 life-size cows made out of plaster that were on exhibit throughout the city. Local artists had the opportunity to purchase a cow, decorate it in any way they wanted to, and exhibit it on the streets of the city. Each individual cow had a theme, and the cows were put up on streets all throughout Manhattan for a few months. During that time, anyone and everyone had access to the cows. In my opinion, Cow Parade is a great example of public art, as well as one of the most exciting and innovative ideas I've seen recently.

Okay ... so we've established that public art is a piece of art that uses its surroundings and is readily available to the public. There's more information on that topic in last night's reading so we won't review it now. But what else is distinctive about public art?

STUDENT B: Well, artists can put up works outside, and use that space to create big works of art that would never fit in a gallery ... like when Christo and Jeanne-Claude put up *The Gates* in Central Park. They hung that saffron-colored material from big doorways—or gates—along 23 miles of the park, and tons of people went to the park to see them. The whole point was that the sunlight would hit the material and it would billow in the wind and it would be beautiful. They could never have found an indoor space that would have created the same effect.

PROFESSOR: I'm glad you brought that up. *The Gates* exhibit is a good example, because it exemplifies a lot of the elements of public art. Something we've already discussed is how public art takes the natural surroundings into account, and works with them. Do you guys know that it took over 20 years for *The Gates* to be approved by New York City, in part because the artists needed to find a way to build the gates without any adverse impact on the environment? That was one of the stipulations of the artists' contract with the city, and they couldn't move the project forward until they solved that dilemma.

Just like *The Gates*, much of the public art we see is controversial. Many people wonder, is it really art to drape a million square yards of fabric across poles in Central Park? Is it really art to spray-paint figures on subway station billboards? Or to paint a couple of plaster cows and park them on street corners in New York City? Or does art need to be more cultured, more refined, more thoughtful than that? We'll get into that discussion a little later though.

So now we've mentioned a few of the factors that need to be present for a work to be called public art. The work has to be fully, and easily, available to the public, either on display outdoors or in an accessible building. The piece should have a synergistic relationship with its surroundings, and it's usually contemporary. Okay, let's go to our books and see what some of our more well-known critics have to say about this subject.

NARRATOR:	Now use your notes to help you answer the questions.
	What is the professor mainly discussing?
	Listen to part of the talk again, and then answer the question.
STUDENT A:	… it's basically any work of art that's readily available to the general population—it's either mounted in an outdoor space, or in a building that's accessible to the public.
PROFESSOR:	So by that definition, wouldn't an exhibit at a museum be public art, because the building is somewhat open to the public? Or is there more to it than that?
NARRATOR:	Why does the professor say this:
PROFESSOR:	Or is there more to it than that?
NARRATOR:	What are two of the key elements that are shared by most works of public art?
	Listen to part of the talk again, and then answer the question.
PROFESSOR:	… that was one of the stipulations of the artists' contract with the city, and they couldn't move the project forward until they solved that dilemma.
NARRATOR:	What does the professor mean when she says this:
PROFESSOR:	… they couldn't move the project forward …
NARRATOR:	Listen to part of the talk again, and then answer the question.
PROFESSOR:	Just like *The Gates*, much of the public art we see is controversial. Many people wonder, is it really art to drape a million square yards of fabric across poles in Central Park? Is it really art to spray-paint figures on subway station billboards? Or to paint a couple of plaster cows and park them on street corners in New York City?
NARRATOR:	How does the professor emphasize the fact that public art is considered controversial?
	Listen to part of the talk again, and then answer the question.
PROFESSOR:	There's more information on that topic in last night's reading so we won't review it now.
NARRATOR:	What can be said about the professor?

Academic Talk 2: Archaeology

Track 4

NARRATOR: Listen to part of a talk in an archaeology class.

PROFESSOR: Okay, yesterday we spoke about how the ancient Egyptians believed in the afterlife. As a result, they wanted to preserve the dead body because they believed the soul would return to it one day and it would need to recognize its own body. The more the dead body looked lifelike, the easier the soul could find it. As you all probably know from TV and the movies, these bodies are called mummies.

So yeah, we all know mummies, but how many of you really understand how complex the process was? Before 1500 B.C., mummification was experimental. It only became more refined between the 18th and 21st Dynasty ... about 1500 to 1000 B.C. Um, don't forget the numbers go backwards when we're talking B.C., okay? After that ... say, 1000 B.C., the process declined. Fortunately, in the fifth century B.C., the Greek historian Herodotus recorded the embalming methods of the Egyptians. Oh, you know the word embalming, right? Preserving the body—and yeah, we have that even today, although not to the degree I'm about to describe.

The first step in mummifying was—and I hope this won't spoil your lunch—removing the brain. The embalmers pulled the brain out through the nose with an iron hook—okay, okay, I know this is a little gross—and then they poured drugs into the skull to preserve it. Archeologists have actually found holes in the bones of a mummy's skull because of this procedure.

Now why did they do that? We all think the brain is the seat of wisdom and knowledge. What would we do without our brain, like the Scarecrow from *The Wizard of Oz*, right? Well, for the ancient Egyptians, the brain was never preserved since they considered it useless. The heart, not the brain, for them was the seat of the soul. Then, as if that weren't enough, the Egyptians would open up the body and remove more organs ... the lungs, intestines, stomach, liver, and spleen. Imagine, all of these were more important than the brain. The heart was always left in place. Because it was the core of a person's character, they believed it was vital for eternal life.

Once the organs were removed, they washed the inside of the body with water and wine. The organs were each wrapped separately in linen and then placed in jars capped with the heads of gods. You remember how many gods the Egyptians worshipped. The jars would later be buried with the body.

Then the body was, was dehydrated for 40 days and washed off with towels. So, because the body was all dried out, it became hard and stiff. The Egyptians actually massaged ... the dry skin with sweet oils and grease. Any cuts were sealed with hot wax. The mouth and nose were filled with cloth, while the body was painted red for men and yellow for women. The arms were arranged across the chest or along the side of the body.

Then, for the next two weeks—imagine, two weeks—the Egyptians would bandage the body with linen strips. Three thousand years later, archeologists discovered the skeletons of two mice that had accidentally nestled inside the bandages and got wrapped up too! Even they got preserved.

Some of the high-ranking mummies had elaborate gold funerary masks placed over their head and shoulders. You've all seen these in books. The poor guys, well they only had cardboard covers. As you can tell, the mummification process was pretty expensive. Only rich people were buried in pyramids—those incredible buildings that housed all the treasures that would then follow them on their final journey. The poor had to accept simple burials, but we can assume they too made the same trip as the rich guys.

That's kind of it in a nutshell. I want to show you some pictures now and review some of the details. Oh, and I also wanted to mention that deliberate embalming of animals was also very common in ancient Egypt—not like the accidental burial of the two mice! Thousands of mummified animals were buried, including sacred animals such as bulls, rams, cats, dogs, ibises, crocodiles, and lots of other species. While animals were honored by the Egyptians—and I'll spend more time tomorrow on the significance of animals in Egyptian mythology—animal mummies haven't always been as venerated as King Tut's was, let's say. In fact, in 1859, a whole graveyard with 300,000 mummified cats was excavated and shipped to Great Britain. Why? To be used as fertilizer.

Okay, so now I'm going to show you some slides of mummies. Could someone turn off the lights, please?

NARRATOR:	Now use your notes to help you answer the questions.
	What is the talk mainly about?
	According to the talk, what did the Egyptians consider the most important organ?
	According to the talk, which of the following can be inferred about Egyptian society?
	Listen to part of the talk again, and then answer the question.
PROFESSOR:	We all think the brain is the seat of wisdom and knowledge. What would we do without our brain, like the Scarecrow from *The Wizard of Oz*, right?
NARRATOR:	Why does the professor say this:
PROFESSOR:	What would we do without our brain …
NARRATOR:	Listen to part of the talk again, and then answer the question.

PROFESSOR:	The embalmers pulled the brain out through the nose with an iron hook—okay, okay, I know this is a little gross—
NARRATOR:	Why does the professor say this:
PROFESSOR:	—okay, okay, I know this is a little gross—
NARRATOR:	In the lecture, the professor describes the steps for mummification. Indicate whether each of the following is a step in this process.

Academic Talk 3: History

Track 5

NARRATOR:	Listen to part of a talk in a history class.
PROFESSOR:	Yesterday, we were discussing some of the economic and political ramifications of the Great Depression, the period that followed the infamous 1929 stock market crash when social, political, and economic factors spurred almost 1,000 bank failures in a 12-month period.

Today we're going to talk about some of the social peculiarities of the same time period, the early 1930s. We'll look at the rise of bank robberies in the thirties and how it was possible for high-profile criminals to bend and shape the American public's opinion of the government and corporate institutions.

So, we've already talked about how the financial crises of the '30s had a negative impact on investor confidence. Whether or not it was true, many Americans felt that mismanagement of funds on the part of financial institutions was the cause of the Great Depression, and, as a result, was the cause of all their misery and hardship. This animosity toward financial institutions created an opportunity for some of the most notorious bank robbers in American history to win over the public. I'm sure you're already familiar with some of these names … John Dillinger, Harry Pierpont, Baby Face Nelson, and Bonnie and Clyde. This, uh, animosity towards banks and big business also gave the public a scapegoat for many of the things that were going wrong with the nation at the time.

What sets these criminals apart from their predecessors is that they somehow managed to win the admire, I mean admiration of the public while stealing their money. Think about it for a minute … while the U.S. public should have been outraged that these criminals were able to walk into a bank, pull a gun on a teller, and walk out with a pile of cash—instead, they turned the thieves into celebrities and then gobbled up the news of their latest daring adventures. Frustrated by bank failures, rampant unemployment, and generally poor economic conditions, many citizens felt that these bank robbers were, were "getting back at" the banks—there was almost a sort of Robin Hood mentality—robbing the banks that robbed the public.

The most infamous of the outlaws was a guy named John Dillinger, a petty criminal who turned to rob, robbing banks after spending eight and a half years in jail for attempting to hold up a grocery store. That's right. He didn't even rob the store. Dillinger confessed in court and was handed an extremely harsh sentence in relation to the crime he had planned to commit. During the time he spent in jail, he made friends with his fellow inmates and eventually hatched a plan to help them all escape from jail as soon as he was freed. It worked. Dillinger and his cohorts, who became known as the Dillinger Gang, then executed several bank robberies during 1933 and 1934.

Dillinger's exploits became so famous that they not only drew the attention of the media and the American public—who treated him like a celebrity—they eventually caught the attention of J. Edgar Hoover. In 1933, Hoover was the head of a brand new government agency called the Federal Bureau of Investigation. Sound familiar? At this point, the public pretty much thought Hoover and the FBI were a joke, and the FBI's attempts to catch Dillinger did nothing to change public opinion at first. But Hoover was determined to catch Dillinger—not only to stop him from robbing banks, but also—and maybe more importantly for Hoover—to earn respect for the FBI.

As the months passed, Dillinger enraged Hoover so much that Hoover began calling him "Public Enemy Number One" and made it his mission to apprehend Dillinger. In reality, Dillinger's ability to slip through the FBI's fingers at every turn made the FBI look inept and unprofessional, which just added to the public's infatuation with Dillinger, and stoked mistrust of the government's new law enforcement agency. Over a month long period in 1935, I'm sorry, it was 1934—in one month in 1934, Dillinger managed to slip through the FBI's fingers four or five times— and every time he escaped, the public just fell more and more in love with him. It's amazing, isn't it? I mean, this guy walks into a bank, steals their savings, and every once in a while, he shoots and kills someone who gets in his way … and the public just eats it up. They treat him like a hero. They're sitting in movie theaters, watching the news, and they applaud him when accounts of his latest robbery show up on the screen.

Anyway, eventually, Hoover and his team captured most of Dillinger's gang and then finally cornered and killed Dillinger in July of 1934, after receiving a tip from his girlfriend. So what had been a fiasco for the FBI turned into their greatest success—after several thwarted efforts, the FBI got their man, and the credibility Hoover was hoping for.

NARRATOR: Now use your notes to help you answer the questions.

What is the main topic of the lecture?

According to the lecture, why was John Dillinger incarcerated?

According to the talk, why did J. Edgar Hoover want to capture John Dillinger?

Why does the professor refer to the previous day's lecture?

Listen to part of the talk again, and then answer the question.

PROFESSOR:	I mean, this guy walks into a bank, steals their savings, and every once in a while, he shoots and kills someone who gets in his way … and the public just eats it up
NARRATOR:	What does the professor suggest?
	According to the discussion, which of the following statements could describe the general feeling of the American public in the 1930s?

Academic Talk 4: Literature

Track 6

NARRATOR:	Listen to part of a talk in a literature class.
PROFESSOR:	Um … If I could have your attention, … uh, let's start today by considering how an author's diction and syntax … or word choice and order … are deliberately chosen in any particular work of literature. Of course, authors, poets, playwrights have a choice of many literary devices. The author creates the structure and an interpreter … or reader … must investigate in order to draw inferences and conclusions.
	Some common literary devices include: symbolism, foreshadowing, characterization, irony, point of view, tone … and so on.
	Symbolism and foreshadowing, which we'll talk about today, require the audience … er … reader to be a bit of a detective … greater inferencing skills are necessary … you know, reading between the lines, understanding what is implied rather than stated. In symbolism, objects seem to stand for something other than themselves. Springtime symbolizes new birth … a tire pump in a garden symbolizes a snake in Eden. Symbolism requires connotation rather than denotation … or figurative rather than literal meaning, as I said, implying rather than stating directly. Typically, to the trained reader, symbolism is easier to see than its not-so-distant cousin, foreshadowing.
	Detecting foreshadowing requires locating suggestions—that's what connotations are—locating suggestions that will appear later in the text. Identifying foreshadowing is particularly satisfying to the reader. The use of foreshadowing creates suspense which is then resolved when the expectation is met. Potentially though, the reader may not be aware of the evidence and clues until the first reading is complete. In other words, the resolution of the plot helps the audience grasp foreshadowing during a subsequent—a second—reading. When a reader rereads … which is expected at the interpretation level … foreshadowing becomes more visible, contributing to the meaning and purpose … plot and … uh, … theme, of the work.
	Now, let's apply this literary device of foreshadowing to specific works. Even the title of a work may indicate foreshadowing. In the case of Susan Glaspell's play entitled *Trifles*. Oh, she also created a short work of prose based on the same plot and theme entitled *A Jury of Her Peers*. The titles alone foreshadow how the tale will be told of a woman being judged by other women based on what appear to be trifles, or insignificant details.

Beyond the title, many works demonstrate foreshadowing in their first lines. How about this? From *A Tale of Two Cities* by Dickens: "It was the best of times, it was the worst of times." The first line gives the reader a glimpse ... er, foreshadowing ... of the happy and tragic events that will be the subject of the novel. In Edgar Allan Poe's "The Tell-Tale Heart," the word choice, sentence length, structure, and repetition provide foreshadowing, even in the speech patterns of the narrator. And Poe also clearly uses foreshadowing in another short story, "The Cask of Amontillado." In that story, a character quite literally declares his intent to seek revenge on his enemy. And since we, as the readers, have already been told what is to happen, given, if you like, ... the, uh ... "whodunit" information, the focus and suspense of the story is thrown onto how the revenge is to be carried out.

There are several examples of foreshadowing here: The revenge takes place in the catacombs, we know that the moment of revenge is approaching as the main character assures his enemy that he will not die of a cough ... Poe is certainly a master of foreshadowing, but he's not the only one who was skilled at using it.

The character of the grandmother in Flannery O'Connor's *A Good Man Is Hard to Find* is a good example. It's almost as if she had a warning, a premonition if you like. The first line, uh, again, is suggestive of bad things to come: "The grandmother didn't want to go to Florida." It is as though she had prophetic knowledge of the events to come.

NARRATOR: Now use your notes to help you answer the questions.

What is the lecture mainly about?

Why does the professor talk about symbolism?

According to the professor, how do symbolism and foreshadowing differ?

Listen to part of the talk again, and then answer the question.

PROFESSOR: Potentially though, the reader may not be aware of the evidence and clues until the first reading is complete.

NARRATOR: What does the professor imply?

What does the professor say about the work *A Jury of Her Peers*?

Listen to part of the talk again, and then answer the question.

PROFESSOR: Poe is certainly a master of foreshadowing, but he's not the only one who was skilled at using it.

NARRATOR: What can be inferred from the professor's statement?

SPEAKING SECTION

Task 1

Track 7

NARRATOR: Task One. For this task, you will be asked to speak about a topic that is familiar to you. You will hear a question. You will then have 15 seconds to prepare your response and 45 seconds to speak.

NARRATOR: Describe the best gift you ever received and say what made the gift so special. Give details to support your choice.

Task 2

Track 8

NARRATOR: Task Two. For this task, you will give your opinion about a topic that is familiar to you. You will hear a question. You will then have 15 seconds to prepare your response and 45 seconds to speak.

NARRATOR: Some students prefer to study alone. Others prefer to study with a friend, or in a group. Which method do you prefer and why? Give details and examples in your explanation.

Task 3

Track 9

NARRATOR: Task Three. Listen to two students as they discuss the announcement.

STUDENT A: Well, at least they're honest.

STUDENT B: How d'you mean?

STUDENT A: I mean it's incredible—absolutely unbelievable—that they'd choose someone who has not, uh, no teaching experience whatsoever. But it just proves that universities today are being run more like businesses than like educational institutions.

STUDENT B: That may not be all bad. I mean, large universities are a lot like businesses. So it's probably good to have someone at the top who understands about budgets and finance and uh, that stuff. Think of all the, the fund-raising a university president has to do ... Senator Mullins's experience in politics and public relations will probably come in handy.

STUDENT A: Senator Mullins's name is sure to raise a lot of money, but I doubt we'll ever see any of it. I hear they're building a new faculty dining room ...

STUDENT B: Well, my friend who works in the financial aid office says they're talking about adding new scholarships. So ... if Mullins can raise enough money, maybe we'll finally get the new science lab they've been talking about for so long. And maybe having a famous president will attract top faculty to the school. That would be a real plus.

NARRATOR: Now get ready to answer the question.

NARRATOR: The woman expresses her opinion of a recent decision made by the university. State her opinion and explain the reasons she gives for holding that opinion.

Task 4

Track 10

NARRATOR: Task Four. Listen to part of a talk in an economics class.

PROFESSOR: There are several reasons why the Bretton Woods system eventually broke down. The success of the system depended to a great extent, on the presence of a dominant player who would be largely responsible for making the rules of the game and making sure those rules were followed. For many years, the United States was that dominant player. Then the 1960s saw Europe and Japan gaining in economic strength, while the United States' economy, in contrast, got steadily weaker. With inflation rising at home, the United States could no longer claim its uh, leadership role, and, uh, eventually, well, the system collapsed when Richard Nixon removed the gold backing from the U.S. dollar in 1971.

But I wouldn't characterize Bretton Woods as a complete failure. It did bring stability to world markets and facilitate increased trade among nations. Indeed, there are some who support a return to the Bretton Woods system in some modified form. Of course, the world is a much different place than it was in 1944. Sixty years ago, no one could have predicted the birth of the euro and the dominant effect its 450-plus million users would have on the world economy. Nevertheless, the fact that Bretton Woods continues to be discussed attests to the very important role that it played in fashioning the world economy after World War II.

NARRATOR: Now get ready to answer the question.

NARRATOR: The professor talked about the end of the Bretton Woods system. Explain what the purpose of the Bretton Woods system was and how and why it ended. Give details and examples to support your answer.

Task 5

Track 11

NARRATOR: Task Five. For this task, you will listen to a dialogue. You will hear a question about it. You will then have 20 seconds to prepare your response and 60 seconds to speak.

Listen to a dialogue between two students. Student A (male): Hey, Sheila? You got a minute?

STUDENT B: Sure, Jack. What's up?

STUDENT A: I, I could use some advice. I'm thinkin' of taking a year off, but I'm just not sure ...

STUDENT B:	What brought this on? You seem to really be enjoying school. I mean, you're always busy …
STUDENT A:	Well, that's sort of the problem. The thing is … Well, to be honest, I didn't do as well first term as I'd hoped and, and I guess I was expecting to get better grades. I was used to being at the top of my class in high school. But here … I guess I wasn't anticipating so much competition …
STUDENT B:	Yeah, but lots of first-year students go through the same thing. Say, have you talked to your advisor about this?
STUDENT A:	Not yet. I'm afraid he's going to tell me to reduce my courseload. And if I do that, I might lose my financial aid, so that's not an option.
STUDENT B:	You know, sometimes it's possible to take an easier course load without necessarily taking fewer credits.
STUDENT A:	Maybe you're right. Still, I can't help thinking I'm just not ready for college. But if I do take a year off, I just don't know what I'd do instead.
STUDENT B:	Well, I had a friend who was in the same boat. She took a year off and got a job. When she finally came back to school, she knew what she wanted to major in, and she was much more enthusiastic about her studies. And the best part was, since she'd been able to put away a little money, she didn't have to work during the academic year. So she was really able to concentrate on her schoolwork and she ended up doing really well.
STUDENT A:	That's kinda what I was hoping to do. But it's such a big step …
NARRATOR:	Now get ready to answer the question.
NARRATOR:	The students discuss possible solutions to the man's problem. Describe the problem. Then state which of the solutions you prefer and explain why.

Task 6

Track 12

NARRATOR:	Task Six. For this task, you will hear a short academic talk. You will hear a question about it. You will then have 20 seconds to prepare your response and 60 seconds to speak. Listen to part of a talk in a marketing class.
PROFESSOR:	Now, the reason that game theory is of interest to so many people is that it combines several different disciplines: mathematics, economics, statistics, and psychology. When you're playing a game, let's say … , um, chess … well, you, uh, you try to come up with a strategy that will result in your winning the game. And part of your strategy will involve trying to outsmart your opponent, trying to guess which move he will make next. Competing businesses operate on the same principle. When two companies are competing for the same objective, they try to guess what the competition's next move will be. In other words, when a company makes decisions—when it tries to choose a strategy to follow—it has to constantly consider what the competition might do in response. And the competition is doing the same thing—constantly trying to figure out what the other side is thinking. Using game-theory terminology, we'd say that

when there are exactly two players and Player A's loss results in Player B's gain … in game theory we call that "zero sum." Of course, things get much more complicated when there are more than two players involved. This all may sound very complex, but the beauty of game theory is that—in principle anyway—it's actually quite simple. In fact, a number of people, among them John Nash, whose name you might be familiar with from the movie, A Beautiful Mind, people like Nash have come up with mathematical formulas that support the idea that many aspects of game theory are, in fact, predict- able. And what's exciting is, once you begin to understand what game theory is all about, you begin to see it at work in everyday life and you see it has applications in so many different and unrelated areas … in sports, in business, in diplomacy. The list is endless.

NARRATOR: Using points and examples from the talk, explain how a price war between two competing retail stores reflects the principles of game theory.

WRITING SECTION

Task 1

Track 13

NARRATOR: Now listen to part of a talk on the topic you just read about.

PROFESSOR: Although scientists cannot predict future temperature trends with 100 percent accuracy, much evidence points to a global warming trend that may eventually make this planet uninhabitable. While there have been large variations in temperature on Earth for thousands of years, the current warming trend is cause for alarm—and we only have ourselves to blame for it.

This is because carbon dioxide—a gas that occurs naturally in the atmosphere—is now produced at alarming rates by industry. Carbon dioxide, or CO_2, is a "greenhouse gas," one of the gases that traps infrared radiation upon release into the atmosphere, making the earth warm enough to support human life.

However, too much greenhouse gas in the atmosphere will cause a radical increase in the surface temperature of the earth. And ever since the Industrial Revolution, the level of greenhouse gas released into the atmosphere has increased dramatically.

So as a result, the temperature of the earth has risen by about one degree over the past century, with accelerated warming in the past two decades. Sure, CO_2 is released naturally into the atmosphere, but it's released at a much higher rate when humans burn solid waste, fossil fuels, and wood products. And this increase will accelerate the natural rate of climate change … scientists expect an increase of up to 10 degrees in the next century.

Some people will try to explain away the global warming trend by saying the recent temperature rise is a natural and cyclical occurrence, but don't let them fool you. It's our industry and emissions that are changing the atmosphere, and only for the worse.

NARRATOR: Summarize the points made in the lecture you just heard, explaining how they cast doubt on points made in the reading.

Task 6

Track 12

NARRATOR: Task Six. For this task, you will hear a short academic talk. You will hear a question about it. You will then have 20 seconds to prepare your response and 60 seconds to speak.

Listen to part of a talk in a marketing class.

PROFESSOR: Now, the reason that game theory is of interest to so many people is that it combines several different disciplines: mathematics, economics, statistics, and psychology. When you're playing a game, let's say ... , um, chess ... well, you, uh, you try to come up with a strategy that will result in your winning the game. And part of your strategy will involve trying to outsmart your opponent, trying to guess which move he will make next. Competing businesses operate on the same principle. When two companies are competing for the same objective, they try to guess what the competition's next move will be. In other words, when a company makes decisions—when it tries to choose a strategy to follow—it has to constantly consider what the competition might do in response. And the competition is doing the same thing—constantly trying to figure out what the other side is thinking. Using game-theory terminology, we'd say that when there are exactly two players and Player A's loss results in Player B's gain ... in game theory we call that "zero sum." Of course, things get much more complicated when there are more than two players involved. This all may sound very complex, but

PROFESSOR: Although scientists cannot predict future temperature trends with 100 percent accuracy, much evidence points to a global warming trend that may eventually make this planet uninhabitable. While there have been large variations in temperature on Earth for thousands of years, the current warming trend is cause for alarm—and we only have ourselves to blame for it.

This is because carbon dioxide—a gas that occurs naturally in the atmosphere—is now produced at alarming rates by industry. Carbon dioxide, or CO_2, is a "greenhouse gas," one of the gases that traps infrared radiation upon release into the atmosphere, making the earth warm enough to support human life.

However, too much greenhouse gas in the atmosphere will cause a radical increase in the surface temperature of the earth. And ever since the Industrial Revolution, the level of greenhouse gas released into the atmosphere has increased dramatically.

So as a result, the temperature of the earth has risen by about one degree over the past century, with accelerated warming in the past two decades. Sure, CO_2 is released naturally into the atmosphere, but it's released at a much higher rate when humans burn solid waste, fossil fuels, and wood products. And this increase will accelerate the natural rate of climate change ... scientists expect an increase of up to 10 degrees in the next century.

Some people will try to explain away the global warming trend by saying the recent temperature rise is a natural and cyclical occurrence, but don't let them fool you. It's our industry and emissions that are changing the atmosphere, and only for the worse.

NARRATOR: Summarize the points made in the lecture you just heard, explaining how they cast doubt on points made in the reading.

PRACTICE TEST 2

LISTENING SECTION

Dialogue 1

Track 14

NARRATOR:	Listen to a dialogue between a student and a peer advisor.
STUDENT:	I'm not sure if I'm in the right office. Is this the peer advisement?
PEER ADVISOR:	It is. Hi, I'm Matt. I'm one of the peer advisors.
STUDENT:	Oh? I didn't see a sign on the door.
PEER ADVISOR:	We're getting a new one. I was just about to stick up a temporary one when you walked in. So, how can I help you?
STUDENT:	Uh, I saw this flyer … here it is … I think I might be interested in the peer advisement program, but I don't know what it is exactly.
PEER ADVISOR:	Well, I can explain. By the way, do you know we have an open house in about three weeks? We started putting up flyers about it.
STUDENT:	Mmm, I only found this general one.
PEER ADVISOR:	Okay. Well, in a nutshell, peer advisement is a great program—for psych majors especially—but anyone can participate since this program trains you. It has coursework to supplement what you get in another major. So what are you majoring in?
STUDENT:	Psych, as a matter of fact.
PEER ADVISOR:	Great. You'll be able to, to overlap some of your classes then with ours. We've got some general courses on counseling methods and a series of seminars and you'll have an internship for a year.
STUDENT:	Where would that be?
PEER ADVISOR:	Everything's done directly on campus. So you'd work right in this office, or maybe in another student-centered office like admissions or the bursar.
STUDENT:	Doing what?
PEER ADVISOR:	Mainly answering students' questions about the college … helping them feel comfortable here … making it easy to understand the requirements. The majority of students who come here are transfers, especially from overseas. Many don't know exactly what to expect from an American college.
STUDENT:	Sounds like a valuable service.
PEER ADVISOR:	It sure is. I actually finished up my program already, but I'm volunteering to help out and I even run one of the seminars now.
STUDENT:	Is there any, uh, like heavy-duty counseling? Like students who might have more, say, major problems?
PEER ADVISOR:	Well, sometimes. You can't avoid that, of course. But if a student needs more in-depth help, we can certainly refer them to someone who can help them. We have access to lots of resources both on and off campus.

STUDENT:	And when did you say the open house was?
PEER ADVISOR:	In about three weeks. Come! If you give me your email address, I can send you a reminder.
NARRATOR:	Now use your notes to help you answer the questions.
	How did the student learn about the peer advisement program?
	Why should the student attend the open house?
	What can be inferred about the peer advisor?
	Listen to part of the dialogue again, and then answer the question.
PEER ADVISOR:	Okay. Well, in a nutshell, peer advisement is a great program—for psych majors especially—but anyone can participate since this program trains you. It has coursework to supplement what you get in another major.
NARRATOR:	What does the peer advisor mean when he says this:
PEER ADVISOR:	Well, in a nutshell …
NARRATOR:	Listen to part of the dialogue again, and then answer the question.
STUDENT:	Is there any, uh, like heavy-duty counseling? Like students who might have more, say, major problems?
PEER ADVISOR:	Well, sometimes. You can't avoid that, of course. But if student needs more in-depth help, we can certainly refer them to someone who can help them.
NARRATOR:	What does the student mean when she says this:
STUDENT:	Is there any, uh, like heavy-duty counseling?

Dialogue 2

Track 15

NARRATOR:	Listen to a dialogue between a student and a bookstore manager.
STUDENT:	May I please speak to, uh, someone in charge of the bookstore?
MANAGER:	That's me. I'm Regina Watson, the manager. What can I do for you?
STUDENT:	I'm a freshman and I'm, I'm looking for work at the college. I was wondering if maybe there's any part-time work available?
MANAGER:	Well, uh, yes, there is, there's a part-time position open at the moment.
STUDENT:	What kind of position is it?
MANAGER:	Mostly cash register work. You've had experience working at a register?
STUDENT:	Yeah, this summer I've been working full-time as a cashier at the Five Star Diner downtown.
MANAGER:	Oh, you did? Why, hmm, I thought you looked familiar. I eat there all the time.
STUDENT:	Well, now that you mention it, I do remember that you used to come in around five—
MANAGER:	Yeah, five, five-thirty. Usually I'd stop by for dinner after work. So, you know what it's like to be working the register at a busy time then …

STUDENT:	Yeah, that I do. Dinner hour gets pretty crowded.
MANAGER:	I'll say. Well, then you can imagine that next week, what with classes starting, this place'll be a madhouse.
STUDENT:	But you only have three registers. How do you manage?
MANAGER:	For about a week and a half, we set up twice as many registers to handle the crowd. Plus we have a returns desk with two registers.
STUDENT:	Sounds like a valuable service.
STUDENT:	Returns? So soon in the semester?
MANAGER:	Oh yes, sometimes students pick up the wrong book by acci-dent, or they decide to drop the course after a couple of classes.
STUDENT:	When things die down, what else would the, uh, job involve?
MANAGER:	Well, we always need somebody at the register, of course, but then there are other responsibilities like inventory, and book orders for the next semester, and sweeping up. Everybody at the register rotates and pitches in.
STUDENT:	I wouldn't mind any of that.
MANAGER:	Well, I'd be happy to consider you. No question we need to hire somebody soon. Could you stop by with a résumé later on today?
STUDENT:	I'm on my way home now and then headed off to work. It's my last week at the diner since my classes are starting next week. Say, maybe I could bring a copy of my résumé to the diner if you're going to stop by?
MANAGER:	Actually, tonight I have to work late to check the stock. Tomorrow'd be just fine, if you could stop by here in the morning.
STUDENT:	No problem. I'll bring my résumé in around eleven.
NARRATOR:	Now use your notes to help you answer the questions.
	Why does the manager think the student looks familiar?
	What can be inferred about the manager?
	Why does the student offer to bring in his résumé tomorrow in the end?
	Listen to part of the dialogue again, and then answer the question.
MANAGER:	… So, you know what it's like to be working the register at a busy time then …
STUDENT:	Yeah, that I do. Dinner hour gets pretty crowded.
MANAGER:	I'll say. Well, then you can imagine that next week, what with classes starting, this place'll be a madhouse.
NARRATOR:	What does the manager mean when she says this:
MANAGER:	… this place'll be a madhouse.
NARRATOR:	Listen to part of the dialogue again, and then answer the question.
MANAGER:	For about a week and a half, we set up twice as many registers to handle the crowd. Plus we have a returns desk with two registers.
STUDENT:	Returns? So soon in the semester?
NARRATOR:	Why is the student surprised?

Academic Talk 1: Music

Track 16

NARRATOR: Listen to part of a talk in a music class.

PROFESSOR: Today I'm going to talk about one of the major influences on musical performance in the 20th and 21st centuries. I mean, of course, the development of sound recording.

Prior to Edison's invention of the phonograph in 1877, musical performances could only be, be described or remembered. They couldn't be reproduced. When sound recording developed, musicians were suddenly able to study the performances of famous musicians in great detail and even to copy them. Musicians who lived outside the major performance centers, such as London, Vienna, Berlin, and Paris could now hear on records how Melba sang or how Kreisler played the violin. Also, minor flaws in the performance that would've been passed over in the concert hall became much more apparent on a recording that could be played over and over again. All of this led performers to concentrate on technical accuracy. And it eroded local performance traditions in favor of a more international style.

Of course, uh, Edison's first idea for exploiting his new invention had nothing to do with music. He saw the phonograph as a dictation machine that would revolutionize the business world. Unfortunately for Edison, many of the office workers who'd painstakingly built up shorthand note-taking skills weren't so keen on the idea … and sabotaged the new dictation machines whenever they could. As a result, very few major firms adopted them.

STUDENT A: So, how'd the phonograph come to be used for recording music?

PROFESSOR: Well, there was a demand from operators of fairgrounds and saloons. They wanted recorded music to entertain customers. And eventually Edison was forced to change direction. Now, given the places where phonograph music was played, it's hardly surprising that the first recordings weren't of Bach and Beethoven. The bestsellers of the day included humorous whistling, cornet solos, and comic dialogues.

STUDENT A: I've heard it said that one of the problems was that Edison wasn't very musical.

PROFESSOR: That is a common view, but I think it does him a bit of an injustice. Although his musical tastes were certainly not highbrow … um … once he was committed to music recording, Edison spent a great deal of time and money building up a collection of American sheet music with an eye to assessing it for its recording potential. His collection runs to tens of thousands of items and is now archived at the University of Michigan.

STUDENT B: So, uh, how did recordings of serious music get started?

PROFESSOR: Well, it took a while. Edison preferred sentimental ballads to opera or chamber music. Plus, the early phonograph had two limitations. One was the poor quality of reproduction and the other was its association with fairgrounds and saloons. Classical artists regarded it as a, um, toy. They simply never took it seriously. However … one artist changed all that … Caruso.

STUDENT A: But wasn't the sound of Caruso's recordings still really terrible? I mean … I've heard a few of those old records and they sound kind of comic.

PROFESSOR: By today's standards that's certainly true, but you've got to remember that people were judging by the standard of cylinder recordings, which were so, so faint that you had to listen through rubber tubes … a bit like today's earphones … to hear anything at all. By 1902, when Caruso made his first recordings, reproduction had improved considerably. Caruso had two great advantages … First, voice recorded very clearly. Remember, the range of that primitive recording apparatus was very limited and many famous artists' voices just didn't suit the equipment.

The other reason was that his interpretations had a certain melodramatic quality … that today we might call larger than life or maybe even exaggerated. Anyway, his style was perfect for overcoming the, uh, limitations of the recording mechanism, and for creating the illusion that he was performing in the room rather than on a machine.

STUDENT B: But that style isn't popular now, is it? These days I don't think artists try to overcome the impersonality of the machine. Most musicians try hard to communicate in concert, but they tend to be much more reserved on CDs.

PROFESSOR: That's a very good point. As recording techniques got more realistic, people I think began to see particular performing conventions as "over the top." Styles that worked well in the heat of the moment in the concert hall, where you had to project and communicate with the person in the back row, maybe started to seem exaggerated when heard repeatedly in the calm of the listener's home. Although it's true that many performers adopt a more extravert style in the concert hall, I think it's also true that some of the perfectionism and "inwardness" of studio performance has spilled over into live performance. We now expect people in concerts to sound like the CD.

NARRATOR: Now use your notes to help you answer the questions.

What is the talk mainly about?

Why does the professor talk about Edison's attempts to market the phonograph as a dictation machine?

Listen to part of the talk again, and then answer the question.

PROFESSOR: Now, given the places where phonograph music was played, it's hardly surprising that the first recordings weren't of Bach and Beethoven.

NARRATOR: What does the professor imply?

What does the professor say about Caruso?

What does the professor say about Edison and music?

According to the talk, which of the following are true of sound recording?

Academic Talk 2: Film History

Track 17

NARRATOR: Listen to part of a talk in a film history class.

PROFESSOR: Okay … We're going to see some clips today from Russian silent cinema, and uh, we're going to use these clips to help us under- stand the art of montage. Montage? If you have never heard of that, I might use the word editing instead. But it's much more than that. Let's see what the great Russian filmmaker from the silent era said about, uh, what can be really called the art of silent film. Film should reflect the truths of life. Maybe you've heard of that concept. Film as truth, film as art. But how does this happen? Eisenstein believed that film was supposed to make … visual connections … connections between contradictory opposites. And this, this would create conflict. And for him, for Eisenstein, conflict was the essence of art. That tension, that sense of problem, to make an important statement. An important message, if you will.

Eisenstein's famous book, it's called Film Form, uh, in it, Eisenstein refers to vibrations of color. He wasn't referring to color in film, because he worked in black and white. But colors in general. Have you ever noticed how when you put a blue and green swatch of color next to each other, the colors seem to change? There's a new visual effect going on. Well, the colors don't actually change, but it's the effect on the mind's eye. What Eisenstein would call their energy or vibrations, interacting with light, plus the receptive eye, and how the brain translates all this stuff … that creates new impressions and new meanings.

Eisenstein's colleague, Kuleshov, applied this same principle. He took a picture of an expressionless actor and juxtaposed it—matched it—to a happy image, like uh, a puppy or a baby. When he showed the two images to a bunch of people, they thought the actor was reacting happily even though, of course, the picture of the actor showed absolutely no emotion! Then he took the same picture of the same actor, and put it next to a sad image, like of a baby crying. What happened? Everybody thought the actor was sad too. But what's really going on? It was the people's association that sad images must mean sad reactions that led them to read into the actor's face.

So, what does all that have to do with editing, or as I mentioned earlier, uh, montage? Eisenstein's controversial principle of montage insists upon the element of conflict arising from this juxtaposition of two or more images. And how one image can lay its meaning on another. The amazing part of this—and the part that's hard to understand in some ways—is that the images colliding editorially do not even have to make sense. You can have a picture of an old person, say, cutting back and forth with a picture of a clock, and that's telling you something about the significance of time to that person … maybe that time is running out … or maybe that the person is waiting for someone. Even though you might never associate the person with the clock right off. The final combination lifts the viewer to a new message of life. A new truth. A new idea. Film as truth, film as art—you're starting to get the idea now, aren't you?

Now, I'll have to throw in another word here. Dialectical. It sounds tough, but if you say a film has a dialectic approach, then, well, what is that? It just means that nothing in life is isolated. Deeper layers of meaning can be extracted from all combined forms. How does this get, um, get translated into film? Dialectical montage ... and you hear, now I'm combining those two words, dialectical and montage. This creates a new "other" from every image that passes before the eye. It's, uh, kind of like a chain reaction of images that build to the film's conclusion.

When you see the clip in a few minutes, for example ... there's a peacock. What do we associate with a peacock? Vanity, arrogance, and the image following it is a man. But what does a peacock have to do with anything? The man lives in the city. How many peacocks live in the city? It's, it's a statement. The man is vain, the man is arrogant. And Eisenstein's driving home the point visually. Let's look at some of these examples on film now.

NARRATOR:	Now use your notes to help you answer the questions.
	What is the talk mainly about?
	What is the overall effect of combining images in a montage?
	Listen to part of the talk again, and then answer the question.
PROFESSOR:	This creates a new "other" from every image that passes before the eye. It's, uh, kind of like a chain reaction of images that build to the film's conclusion.
NARRATOR:	What can be inferred from this comment by the professor:
PROFESSOR:	It's, uh, kind of like a chain reaction of images ...
NARRATOR:	Listen to part of the talk again, and then answer the question.
PROFESSOR:	Everybody thought the actor was sad too. But what's really going on?
NARRATOR:	Why does the professor say this:
PROFESSOR:	But what's really going on?
NARRATOR:	Listen to part of the talk again, and then answer the question.
PROFESSOR:	Well, the colors don't actually change, but it's the effect on the mind's eye.
NARRATOR:	What does the professor mean when she says this:
PROFESSOR:	... but it's the effect on the mind's eye.
NARRATOR:	Which of the following does the professor compare film to in the lecture?

Academic Talk 3: History

Track 18

NARRATOR:	Listen to part of a lecture in a history class.
PROFESSOR:	Let's take a look at the history of the holiday that's coming up in a couple of weeks: New Year's Day. New Year's is probably the oldest ongoing

holiday in human history. The Babylonians, way back in 2000 B.C., first observed it on the full moon nearest the spring equinox, and this without even the benefit of a written calendar. The date we use today—January 1st—was a long time coming. It's only been the official start of the "new" year for the last four centuries, since 1582. But we'll get to that later. The ancient Persians and Egyptians considered the beginning of their new year to be the autumnal equinox on September 21st. This coincided with the annual flooding of the Nile River . . . a very important time, of course, and worthy of a new year. The Greeks opted for the summer solstice on June 21st, while the Romans . . . like the Babylonians . . . preferred the vernal—or spring—equinox around March 25th.

Each civilization celebrated this rebirth—this beginning of a new year—over a period of several days, usually with ritualistic festivities. The Babylonians used to decapitate statues to symbolize the end of the old year. Fortunately, we haven't carried over that tradition. But as you can see, based on the different seasonal dates, the concept of the New Year . . . for these ancient civilizations . . . revolved around agriculture. And rightly so. Without the "newborn" products of the earth, they'd never have survived.

In 153 B.C., however, the beginning of the New Year temporarily shifted to January 1st, and it wasn't even tied to a specific harvest season. The month itself was named for the Roman god Janus, the god of change . . . and . . . recognize the name January there, right? Now, Janus had two faces, so you could imagine the old and the new, coming and going, as he guarded the doorway. This made him perfect for commemorating a new year when the old and the new comes and goes.

Over time, the church, uh, prohibited the wild celebrations that went with the pagan January 1st holiday. To give credence to this prohibition, they attached religious significance to the days following Christmas. In A.D. 567 the medieval Roman Catholic Church's Council of Tours went a step further and abolished January 1st as the New Year and the date reverted back to March 25th, to coincide with the new life of spring. Makes sense for a new year, doesn't it?

Then, once again, the church intervened, and in 1582 Pope Gregory XIII changed the way the world marked time, once and for all, with the adoption of the Gregorian calendar. And so . . . the date for the New Year returned to the month of the two-faced god.

Through the ages, the midnight hour's always been, been powerful and mysterious. What happens during those seconds of transition from one year to the next is often thought to color what comes in the following year. December 31st was an opportunity for individuals to make their first step into the New Year the best. In some traditions, the first step was a literal one. People held ceremonies where they unbarred the front door of their home to welcome guests. Scotland, for example, did "first-footing" on New Year's Eve. The first person stepping upon a threshold at the stroke of midnight was seen as an omen for the coming year.

Hopefully, it was a friendly person bearing gifts.

In the U.S., New Year's celebrants—known as mummers—used to shoot in the New Year with guns and shouting. They dressed up in costumes and visited one house after another, entertaining everybody with impersonations and then, uh, accepting cakes and ale in return.

Up through the mid-19th century, visiting for the New Year was a great social event, almost a competition ... who could visit the most in the fewest number of hours? Ladies tried to outdo each other in attracting the finest guests, guests who sometimes made 80 calls in one day. Each attempting to be the "first" over the threshold.

This was certainly one way to invite good fortune: promise a good time, with lots of noise and fun to scare off trouble. And there's still no better way to celebrate a new year, in my opinion.

NARRATOR:	Now use your notes to help you answer the questions.
	What is the lecture mainly about?
	Where did the name of the first month come from?
	What can be inferred about the earliest dates for the New Year?
	Listen to part of the talk again, and then answer the question.
PROFESSOR:	In A.D. 567 the medieval Roman Catholic Church's Council of Tours went a step further and abolished January 1st as the New Year and the date reverted back to March 25th, to coincide with the new life of spring. Makes sense for a new year, doesn't it?
NARRATOR:	Why does the professor say this:
PROFESSOR:	Makes sense for a new year, doesn't it?
NARRATOR:	According to the talk, which of the following is true of the New Year's holiday?
	Listen to part of the talk again, and then answer the question.
PROFESSOR:	The first person stepping upon a threshold at the stroke of midnight was seen as an omen for the coming year. Hopefully, it was a friendly person bearing gifts.
NARRATOR:	What does the professor mean when she says this:
PROFESSOR:	Hopefully, it was a friendly person bearing gifts.

Academic Talk 4: Physics

Track 19

NARRATOR:	Listen to a part of a talk in a physics class.
PROFESSOR:	Okay, today, we're going to talk about batteries. Now, as you know, uh, batteries are used throughout the world as portable sources of electrical power in products such as, uh, CD players, laptop computers, power tools, and, uh, even electric vehicles. In fact, anytime the need for portability outweighs the higher cost of portable energy, people turn to

batteries. Now, the downside to batteries is their higher cost—batteries currently cost over a thousand times the price of the power you get from the wall sockets in your home. Yet these higher costs don't seem to stop people from buying more and more batteries.

So … okay, let's get to the important stuff … how does a battery work? Now, uh, a battery is made up of one or more devices known as red-ox cells. That's R-E-D dash O-X, short for *reduction and oxidation*, which is what happens inside.

Okay, so, what's a red-ox cell? Well, you've heard the saying, "There're two kinds of people in this world—givers and takers." This may help describe what red-ox cells are and how they work. In red-ox cells, what is being given and taken are electrons—those are, of course, the tiny negatively charged particles that fly around the nucleus of all atoms. Commonly used red-ox cells contain two different electrodes. The first is an electron donor—uh, it releases electrons. The second electrode accepts these electrons. The material giving up electrons is called the anode, you spell that A-N-O-D-E, while the, uh, the material that takes these electrons is called the cathode. Cathode is spelled C-A-T-H-O-D-E.

So, a red-ox cell consists of three basic materials: an anode and a cathode in one container, and a conducting substance between them. This conducting substance is called an electrolyte—it carries the electrons from anode to cathode. A number of substances can act as the electrolyte. In the earliest batteries, the electrolyte was a liquid, such as sulfuric acid. You can still see this in today's car batteries. Later, in order to make batteries more convenient and portable, this liquid was replaced by a paste—that's how we got the dry cell or flashlight battery, which was first patented in 1866. The main advantage of a dry cell battery is that it's a lot easier to transport than a battery that uses a liquid as its electrolyte.

Regardless of what is used as the electrolyte, the process inside a battery is the same. The electrons flow from the anode to the cathode through the electrolyte and back to the anode through a wire or other connector outside the cell. All you need to do is connect this wire—complete the circuit outside the battery so that the electrons can get back to the anode.

So how much power do you get from a battery? Well that depends on two important concepts, current and voltage. The current is the number of electrons that flow around the circuit, whereas the voltage is the pressure with which they flow. The pressure of the electron flow in the circuit depends on the materials used for the anode and cathode. These materials determine how fast the anode can get rid of electrons and how fast the cathode can accept them.

An easy way to imagine the potential difference in a battery is to think of a water pipe. In a water pipe the power depends both on how strong the pressure is and how much water is flowing through the pipe, and it's exactly the same with an electric current. To determine the total power, you multiply the pressure by the amount of current. This power is measured in watts, named after the British scientist, James Watt. You can increase the power by increasing the current in one cell—that is by increasing the surface area of cathode and anode available to exchange electrons, or simply by connecting several cells together.

NARRATOR: Now use your notes to help you answer the questions.

What is the main topic of the lecture?

What does the professor imply?

Listen to part of the talk again, and then answer the question.

PROFESSOR: Okay, so, what's a red-ox cell? Well, you've heard the saying, "There're two kinds of people in this world—givers and takers."

NARRATOR: Why does the professor refer to givers and takers?

According to the professor, why is the dry cell battery better than earlier batteries?

Why does the professor use the example of the water pipe?

According to the lecture, which of the following are true of batteries?

SPEAKING SECTION

Task 1

Track 20

NARRATOR: Task One. For this task, you will be asked to speak about a topic that is familiar to you. You will hear a question. You will then have 15 seconds to prepare your response and 15 seconds to speak.

NARRATOR: Describe a place you like to visit and explain why you like it.

Include details and give examples to support your explanation.

Task 2

Track 21

NARRATOR: Task Two. For this task, you will give your opinion about a topic that is familiar to you. You will hear a question. You will then have 15 seconds to prepare your response and 45 seconds to speak.

NARRATOR: Some people like to socialize with a group of people. Other people like to spend time alone. Which way do you prefer to spend your free time? Include details and examples in your explanation.

Task 3

Track 22

NARRATOR: Task Three. Listen to two students as they discuss the change in policy.

STUDENT A: Why is it that the commuters are always getting discriminated against?

STUDENT B: I think the new system's a good idea. At least everyone'll have a fair shot. The faculty won't get special treatment.

STUDENT A: It's the commuters who deserve special treatment. Most of the professors live pretty close by. For those of us who live far away from campus, convenience is a necessity. Now, we'll have to waste precious study time driving around in circles. Or worse yet, we'll have to pay some garage.

STUDENT B: You can't really say we don't get special treatment. The annual fee we pay for a permit's a lot lower than what the faculty pays.

STUDENT A: At least, under the old system, we were guaranteed spots till they ran out. Now, I'll be competing with everyone, including people who live on campus. Under this new policy, I'll just have to hope I get lucky.

STUDENT B: You know, my brother's school instituted a similar system last year. For some reason, a lot of people didn't even bother entering. So who knows? Maybe we'll actually have a better chance than before …

NARRATOR: Now get ready to answer the question.

NARRATOR: The woman expresses her opinion about a new university policy. State her opinion and explain the reasons she gives for holding that opinion.

Task 4

Track 23

NARRATOR:	Task Four. Listen to part of a talk in an economics class.
PROFESSOR:	The 19th-century Corn Law of Britain is interesting to look at because it mirrors some of the trade issues that continue to affect politics today. As you will recall from your reading, bread prices went way up in England during the wars with France. But even though people weren't fond of paying high prices for their daily bread, there was a war on, difficulties were expected, and the people shrugged and bore it. But when the war ended, and Parliament acted to keep those prices up, the reaction was very different. In fact, as the legislation was being passed, Parliament had to be defended by troops against a crowd that had gathered to express their, uh, opposition to the law.
	This law was opposed by different segments of the population for different reasons. At this point in British history, towns were growing, and the former farmers who moved to the towns to work in industry no longer had access to their own fresh food. They were increasingly dependent on bread—and the more money they spent on bread, the less they had for their rent and everything else.
	Now, the manufacturers who created the jobs in the towns hated the law because they thought higher bread prices would lead to demands for higher wages—and they saw it as a symbol of the political dominance of the landowners. That is to say, Parliament was listening to the landowners, and not to the new manufacturers.
	Opposition to the law did not let up, and it went through a series of reforms. But despite the size of the first opposition group, and the wealth of the second, it wasn't repealed until the 1840s.
NARRATOR:	Now get ready to answer the question.
NARRATOR:	The professor discusses the Corn Law. Using information from the lecture and the reading, explain why the Corn Law was enacted, and why some people opposed it.

Task 5

Track 24

NARRATOR:	Task Five. For this task, you will listen to a dialogue. You will hear a question about it. You will then have 20 seconds to prepare your response and 60 seconds to speak.
	Listen to a dialogue between two students.
STUDENT A:	That was such a great speech! I really wish I could work on her campaign.
STUDENT B:	If you believe in her that much, why don't you go for it?
STUDENT A:	I'd love to, but I've got a job. It's not that I make that much money, but the references'll come in handy when I start job hunting.

STUDENT B:	You probably wouldn't make much money working on a campaign either, but I bet a recommendation from a political candidate would look a lot more impressive than a recommendation from a book- store.
STUDENT A:	Yeah, but I've been working at the bookstore for such a long time. I wouldn't want to leave the manager stranded just when a new term's about to start. Besides, it's a pretty easy job. On slow nights, I can usually get some schoolwork done. I couldn't get away with that if I worked on a political campaign. My cousin worked on one last summer and she said things were always busy … always hectic.
STUDENT B:	It sounds like the kind of thing you'd enjoy. You seem happiest when you've got to juggle a lot of responsibilities. Remember how much you enjoyed organizing that fund-raiser last year?
STUDENT A:	You're probably right. But it'd be so time-consuming working on a political campaign. As it is, I barely have time to hang out with my friends.
STUDENT B:	Just think of all the people you'd meet … It'd be great for your social life!
STUDENT A:	Maybe I'll join the campaign during the summer, when I've got more time to spare.
STUDENT B:	Who knows if she'll still be a candidate this summer? If you really want to help Miller's campaign, you should go down there right now, when she needs your help the most.
STUDENT A:	You're starting to sound like a politician yourself … Why don't you consider running for office?
NARRATOR:	Now get ready to answer the question.
NARRATOR:	The woman tries to persuade the man to do something. Say what she tries to persuade him to do and explain the reasons she gives.

Task 6

Track 25

NARRATOR:	Task Six. For this task, you will hear a short academic talk. You will hear a question about it. You will then have 20 seconds to prepare your response and 60 seconds to speak.
	Listen to part of a talk in an urban history class.
PROFESSOR:	Usually, when people talk about the Harlem Renaissance—the period extending from the end of World War I to the Great Depression in the mid-1930s—they focus on the cultural aspects, and particularly on the great black writers of the period who produced an extensive body of literature of all types: drama, poetry, fiction, and nonfiction.
	Certainly, culture was an important part of the rebirth of this New York neighborhood. But there's another element of the Harlem Renaissance that can't be ignored, and without which this rebirth would never have come about, and that is the economic aspect. Blacks began settling in the

northern cities of the United States soon after the end of the Civil War. This migration to the North was the result of a variety of factors. Blacks were eager to escape the racism and discrimination they suffered in the South. At the same time, with the South in the midst of an economic depression, blacks saw the North as the land of opportunity.

Before it became the social and cultural center of black America, Harlem was a white, upper-class neighborhood inhabited by a large number of Jews and Italians. Thanks in large part to huge improvements in public transportation—the advent of the bus and the elevated train—Harlem enjoyed a real estate boom, which spurred a big surge in construction. Then, suddenly, between 1903 and 1905, an economic crisis brought a sudden end to the construction, leaving many homes and apartment buildings abandoned and unfinished. At about this same time, the subway line that connected Harlem to downtown Manhattan was completed. The existence of convenient public transportation and the availability of affordable housing were two factors that paved the way for blacks to move into Harlem in large numbers.

NARRATOR: Now get ready to answer the question.

NARRATOR: Using points and examples from the talk, explain how economic factors contributed to the Harlem Renaissance in New York City in the early 1900s.

WRITING SECTION

Task 1

Track 26

NARRATOR: Listen to part of a talk on the topic you just read about.

PROFESSOR: We talked earlier about the nativist view of language acquisition shared by Lenneberg and Chomsky … that language learners use an innate "language acquisition device" to help them learn a language. Nativists theorize that the critical period for learning a language is some- where between age 2 and 13 or 14, at which point our brains change, making it nearly impossible to ever again achieve native-like proficiency in a second language.

But how many of you know of people who've learned a second language as adults and can speak it really well? And how do the nativists' theories explain a student who begins learning a foreign language at age 10 but never really becomes proficient? Shouldn't their internal "language acquisition device" kick in … since their brains haven't changed yet? Nativists suggest that biological factors rule language learning, but there are other schools of thought as well.

Some modern linguists—called "environmentalists"—believe that the environment in which a student is taught determines how well he or she learns a language. John Schumann argues that students who don't have the opportunity … or the desire … to practice speaking the language, won't learn the language … regardless of age or ability. He says it's especially beneficial if language learners can practice speaking with native speakers … perhaps even integrate into a community where the language is spoken.

Environmentalists believe that the crucial element of language learning is the interaction that learners have with the language, whether this interaction takes place with other speakers of the language or with input from other sources like television or radio. But what's crucial … is that the more often learners hear and speak the language, the more successful they'll be in understanding the language.

NARRATOR: Summarize the main points in the lecture you just heard, explaining how they cast doubt on the points made in the reading.

PRACTICE TEST 3

LISTENING SECTION

Dialogue 1

Track 27

NARRATOR:	Listen to a dialogue between a student and a professor.
PROFESSOR:	Well, Marie, I appreciate you coming in on such short notice.
STUDENT:	It's no problem, Professor Chen. I spend almost every day here on campus. I … I practically feel like I live here.
PROFESSOR:	Hmm, then you might not want to take on this research position after all.
STUDENT:	Oh! Oh, no, I didn't mean it that way, Professor Chen. I just meant I'm around the college a lot between classes … and now, working for you … hopefully.
PROFESSOR:	I put in long hours myself as an undergrad, you know, back in the Dark Ages. Anyway, so do you think you'll be able to devote about 10 hours a week to being my research assistant?
STUDENT:	Yes, of course. I'm looking forward to it … I was very grateful when you called to ask if I'd be interested in the job.
PROFESSOR:	Well, I was looking through the papers that your class did for me last semester, and yours was outstanding. You really paid attention to detail with your research. That's the kind of precision work I'm looking for.
STUDENT:	So, what would my responsibilities be?
PROFESSOR:	First off, I'm working on a textbook on bilingual education, so I'd need you to check the databases for every current journal article that's out there … I'll let you read the book prospectus before you start and you'll see exactly what focus I'm after.
STUDENT:	I can definitely manage that. I love doing database searches and checking out websites.
PROFESSOR:	Good. Although I mention that first, it's not my number-one priority. A more pressing project is entering the data I just collected from my study on students' attitudes toward test taking—I assume you remember the spreadsheet program that you used in my class last year?
STUDENT:	Oh, yeah. I use that program in two of my classes this semester.
PROFESSOR:	Well, then, I'll be giving you about 200 questionnaires and you'll need to enter those data, according to the codes I indicate.
STUDENT:	When would you like me to start doing the data entry?
PROFESSOR:	I'm expecting the first batch of 50 questionnaires this afternoon, and you could start—well, we need to set up your schedule, don't you think? Can we do that tomorrow during my office hours? I have to run to a meeting now.
STUDENT:	That sounds fine.

PROFESSOR:	Great. And I'll have a key made for you at some point. I'm here every day, but sometimes I go out of town.
STUDENT:	Every day, like me.
PROFESSOR:	Yes, sometimes I feel like I live here too!
NARRATOR:	Now use your notes to help you answer the questions.
	How does the professor know the student?
	Why does the professor think the student could work well with him?
	What does the professor want the student to do first?
	What can be inferred about most of the work the student will have to do?
	Listen to part of the dialogue again, and then answer the question.
STUDENT:	I spend almost every day here on campus. I … I practically feel like I live here.
PROFESSOR:	Hmm, then you might not want to take on this research position after all.
NARRATOR:	What does the professor imply when he says this:
PROFESSOR:	Hmm, then you might not want to take on this research position after all.

Dialogue 2

Track 28

NARRATOR:	Listen to a dialogue between a first-year student and his advisor.
STUDENT:	I really appreciate your taking the time to see me.
ADVISOR:	Let's see if I can help. What's this about? Student: I … I think I really need to drop a course, but I feel bad. Advisor: Why's that?
STUDENT:	I feel bad because I hate giving up … it's just not my nature to quit in the middle of something.
ADVISOR:	I understand. But what makes you want to drop it?
STUDENT:	I … I don't like the way the professor's teaching … I hate to say that.
ADVISOR:	Tell me what's going on.
STUDENT:	It sounds like I'm complaining, but I mean, look at my grades. I have all A's, a 4.0 GPA. It's not like I'm trying to weasel out of work.
ADVISOR:	Not with all A's, I wouldn't think.
STUDENT:	I mean, the professor rambles a lot, gets off-topic, you know. He starts with one idea and 10 minutes later he's somewhere else.
ADVISOR:	That can be disconcerting.
STUDENT:	And he gave us a list of stuff for the midterm, but practically nothing from the list was on the test. In fact, there were questions I swear he never talked about in class.
ADVISOR:	Hmm, I see the problem, but my question is, is this a required course?
STUDENT:	No, that's the irony. I was just taking it because I wanted to learn more about the topic. It's like a personal interest.

ADVISOR:	Well, this is a little easier to handle because it's not a requirement. As an elective, you're free to drop it.
STUDENT:	There's no penalty for dropping, is there?
ADVISOR:	No. That is, not yet, because fortunately, you're just under the wire for the deadline. It will go on your record as a WD—a withdrawal, but that won't affect your GPA.
STUDENT:	Whew.
ADVISOR:	So go to the Registrar and ask for the form. Or better yet—since you don't want to wait too long—drop it online.
STUDENT:	I'm gonna go to the library now and do it. Like I said, I really wanted to stick with this course to the end, but when I saw that 65 on my midterm, I said forget it.
ADVISOR:	Well, maybe you could audit the course?
STUDENT:	Oh, I, I—no, I just can't take it with this guy!
ADVISOR:	Well, maybe you can take the course in the future with a professor whose teaching style is more in tune with your learning style.
STUDENT:	Yeah, I've got three more semesters to go, so I guess that's a possibility.
NARRATOR:	Now use your notes to help you answer the questions.
	What is the student's main concern with the course he wants to drop?
	Why did the student think the midterm exam was unusual?
NARRATOR:	Now use your notes to help you answer the questions.
	Why does the advisor say the student can drop the course now?
	What can be inferred as the main reason the student asked about dropping the course?
	Listen to part of the dialogue again, and then answer the question.
STUDENT:	… It's not like I'm trying to weasel out of work.
ADVISOR:	Not with all A's, I wouldn't think.
NARRATOR:	What does the advisor mean?

Academic Talk 1: Women's Studies

Track 29

NARRATOR:	Listen to part of a talk in a women's studies class.
PROFESSOR:	Sometimes, in order to understand the development of the feminist movement in one culture, it's useful to compare and contrast it with that in another culture. By taking two very different cultures—the U.S. and India, for example—we can see some of the motivations behind their respective feminist movements. First, let me ground you in a little background of India's history as it relates to women's issues.
	One researcher called the Indian women's movement a complicated process. It was born out of the country's independence, declared in 1947. Its constitution called for equality between men and women. Let me make an aside here … although I'm not focusing on the U.S. now—

STUDENT A: I was just gonna say, it reminds me of the U.S. Constitution. Even though it was written in the 18th century, it didn't even really mention women's rights until the women's voting amendment was added in the 20th century.

PROFESSOR: You just made my point, and I'll let you all think about that one for a moment. Getting back to India though, uh, India established a number of administrative bodies designed to create opportunities for women. So with this, India established a promising foundation for equal- ity that, that facilitated women's activism, especially in the 1970s. Can anyone tell me why that decade's so important to feminism?

STUDENT B: I seem to remember that in the '70s, as we spoke about in, uh, was it last week? The United Nations declared 1975 International Women's Year.

STUDENT A: Could you also say that in the '70s the women's movement became known all around the globe?

PROFESSOR: Yes, and we'll be looking at other countries to see some interesting parallels. Early feminism in India was rooted in social conditions that affected quality of life for both men and women. People often forget that women were concerned for the welfare of their sons and husbands too. When people think of "quote" women's lib in the U.S., for example, we often get strong—and may I add, misleading—images that don't accurately portray the women's movement.

STUDENT B: I think most people—and me too, once upon a time—most people think of tough, angry women screaming for equality.

PROFESSOR: And for many people, that became the stereotypical women's libber, at least in the U.S. But that's far from the truth. In India and elsewhere, women were indeed concerned about equality in general, and challenged exploitative, extortionist practices by landowners, for example. Of course, they also turned to critical issues affecting women's safety and health. Concerned about the effects of alcohol in the home environment, Indian women sometimes took the law into their own hands. Like, they would destroy liquor stores that contributed to drinking problems.

Very important—Indian women participated in numerous episodes of mass solidarity. This suggests that they'd developed effective campaigns for, for communication and shared belief. For example, as demonstrations of women marched through a village, women in the homes would come out beating their utensils, like metal plates with rolling pins, in a nonverbal outcry of support.

STUDENT B: Better to beat plates than people!

PROFESSOR: Good point. The Indian women's movement matured during the 1980s. Sisterhood was celebrated in a specifically Indian context, emphasizing positive aspects of women's creativity and potential. A national workshop featured feminists and artists who explored important women's topics through theater, song and dance, and fine arts. They tapped many traditions ... religion, mythology, and Indian culture ... for symbols of women's power.

STUDENT A:	They must have chosen a lot of women warriors and goddesses, all of them pretty powerful figures.
PROFESSOR:	And these images represented their struggles and, uh, vitality. One writer called the reach of the Indian women's movement both vertical and horizontal. In other times, rather, in other words, the movement spanned a variety of organizations on the foundational level, and also reached up into the highest echelons of governance. Equally important to the movement was the representation of women from rural and urban settings at conferences. Today, Indian women's groups are joining movements in the U.S. and Britain because many Indian women are resettling in those countries.
	Later this week, I'll describe some of the more controversial social traditions unique to India that seriously challenged the women's movement for two decades, and continue to do so. Although I already made some parallels to the U.S. feminist movement, I'll synthesize the comparison of both countries after we address more aspects of Indian culture. Please jot down in your notes any parallels you might see between the two countries, based on our previous discussions of the U.S. women's movement.
NARRATOR:	Now use your notes to help you answer the questions.
	What is the talk mainly about?
	How did Indian village women show their support for demonstrators?
	What can be inferred about the Indian women's movement from the 1970s to 1980s?
	Listen to part of the talk again, and then answer the question.
PROFESSOR:	Let me make an aside here … although I'm not focusing on the U.S. now—
NARRATOR:	Why does the professor say this:
PROFESSOR:	Let me make an aside here …
NARRATOR:	Listen to part of the talk again, and then answer the question.
STUDENT B:	I think most people—and me too, once upon a time—most people think of tough, angry women screaming for equality.
NARRATOR:	What does the student mean when she says this:
STUDENT B:	—and me too, once upon a time—
NARRATOR:	In the talk, the professor describes a number of facts that are part of the Indian women's movement. Indicate which of the following were mentioned in the talk.

Academic Talk 2: Film Studies

Track 30

NARRATOR:	Listen to part of a talk in a film studies class.
PROFESSOR:	Editing is a vital component of the film process, but I bet few people really know how complicated it is. Now, why do I say that? Well, everyone knows the big names … actors, directors, producers … what we call the names above the title. But how many of you can name a film editor? Think about this the next time you see an awards show. Who notices the editing category?
STUDENT A:	Isn't that one of the awards they give early in the program? Like, I know the movies … but editors?
STUDENT B:	I always say, who are those people, and when are the big awards coming?
PROFESSOR:	Exactly. The "big" awards. But next time you want to say that, stop and think. If it weren't for editors, we wouldn't even have movies. Sure the actors and directors and writers are important. But who's putting those pieces of film together? Who sat at the old Moviola machine passing film strips through and splicing them together? Okay, yes, today everything's computerized, but the same principles still apply. Some creative individual sits down with a mountain of shots, which become scenes and sequences, and decides how to put it all together. That's the editor.
STUDENT A:	But what's the big deal? That's more like a technical thing. Like organizing papers in a file or something. The director's got all the big ideas.
PROFESSOR:	Granted, the director's a visionary. But editors work very closely with directors and can influence them.
STUDENT B:	Come to think of it, I've heard something like … editors can make or break a film, or important scenes sometimes end up on the cutting room floor. Sounds like the editor can be pretty powerful.
PROFESSOR:	Definitely. Editors work so closely with the film, they can see nuances more objectively than the director sometimes. Editors organize minutiae. They intensify subtleties. They heighten emotions. Editors blend countless elements of image and sound to create a film experience for an audience. Incredibly, their work's not always visible. Some editors want their work to be what they call seamless … without obvious visible connections. They want the effect of their work to be subliminal. What does that mean?
STUDENT A:	Uh, manipulative?
STUDENT B:	That's too negative. I'd say getting a point across to the audience without them even knowing what's happening. Sneaky in a good way.
PROFESSOR:	You're both right. As you watch a film, do you ever think—I mean, consciously think—okay, I just saw the woman go to the phone. Cut. There's the phone close up. Cut. There's a shot of her putting the receiver to her mouth and she talks. Cut to the person calling her … I know I don't think about those pieces of film unless I sit down and analyze each and every frame.

Instead, we see this sequence of shot after shot after shot, and we feel the woman's curiosity as she answers the phone, or maybe her dread when we know someone is harassing her. Of course, we get clues from the actor's face … the lighting, even the music playing underneath. But we feel suspense in seeing the phone by itself and the woman's hand reaching into the shot to pick it up. In less than five seconds, the editor decides to show you four separate shots that he or she considered important enough to cut together … in just that order, in those brief moments, with sound effects or music or maybe only silence. So many choices, you see, to create an impression, an emotion, a sense of movement and energy by joining shots together.

STUDENT B: So it is kind of manipulating our emotions, like he said, but—

STUDENT A: But yeah, like she said, it's a good kind of manipulation, like sneaking up on us for a positive effect.

PROFESSOR: Uh, usually. Film manipulates our emotions all the time and for different purposes. Editors are happy when you don't notice that the shots are all linked up and you can focus on the story. A good editor makes every shot count. I've heard that some editors can spend hours debating whether one shot needs to be two frames longer or shorter. Two frames, imagine! For them, two frames too long, and the rhythm of the scene's ruined. Two frames less, and the scene might have just the right punch to make you jump out of your seat.

STUDENT A: Man! We can't even see two frames with our naked eye when it's projected, but it must be important if they spend all that time on it.

PROFESSOR: We're actually going to compare some clips with extra frames, and see if the editor's right to chop them out. If you come away with anything after that—

STUDENT A: It's to pay attention to the "Best Editing" awards!

NARRATOR: Now use your notes to help you answer the questions.

What is the talk mainly about?

According to the talk, which of the following are two aspects of a film editor's job?

What can be inferred about the editor's job?

Listen to part of the talk again, and then answer the question.

PROFESSOR: Editing is a vital component of the film process, but I bet few people really know how complicated it is. Now, why do I say that?

NARRATOR: What is the purpose of the professor asking this question:

PROFESSOR: Now, why do I say that?

NARRATOR: Listen to part of the talk again, and then answer the question.

STUDENT B: So it is kind of manipulating our emotions, like he said, but—

STUDENT A: But yeah, like she said, it's a good kind of manipulation, like sneaking up on us for a positive effect.

NARRATOR: What are the students implying?

Listen to part of the talk again, and then answer the question.

PROFESSOR: Two frames less, and the scene might have just the right punch to make you jump out of your seat.

NARRATOR: Why does the professor say this:

PROFESSOR: ... the scene might have just the right punch ...

Academic Talk 3: Music

Track 31

NARRATOR: Listen to part of a talk in a music class.

PROFESSOR: Perhaps not many of you've heard of Joules Graves, but I hope you listened to her songs for that was part of the homework. Her CD, *A Sacred Tantrum*, specifically addresses women's perceptions. Both how women are perceived and how they should be perceived. At the same time, though, Graves talks about the human condition. Loving, healing, dancing, contemplating. Being lost and being found. Anger and loneliness.

STUDENT A: Sounds like she just about covers everything a person could go through in life ... both men and women.

PROFESSOR: Yes, you hit the nail on the head. Graves depicts a realistic emotional journey for everyone. She thinks people shouldn't be afraid to look at themselves. Even if they feel angry, they can rediscover something sacred about themselves in relation to nature. Graves uses the metaphor of water to help convey her nature theme. But why water?

STUDENT B: Water is soothing and calming. And it cleans.

STUDENT A: And it's used a lot in literature, as a symbol for life. Like, aren't people always searching for signs of water on other planets as evidence of life?

PROFESSOR: Exactly. And aren't babies born in water? And life was said to spring from water? We equate water with life. So Graves is saying how water can heal someone who's angry or been hurt by negative social constructs. She uses the water idea as a way to crash—not literally, of course—through such social constructs as fashion, gender, and the prim-and-proper way society thinks women should behave.

STUDENT B: Well, I heard that people refer to the women's movement over the last 150 years as happening in waves, like the first wave, second wave, third wave.

STUDENT A: What do waves have to do with it?

STUDENT B: Think about waves on a beach and how they come crashing down with force ...

PROFESSOR: And the women's movement did just that. It crashed down— so to speak—on some of those social constructs. Graves makes no small connection between the feminist movement and the water in her songs. And we hear the final songs on the CD repeat the major themes she weaves throughout the CD: anger giving way to self-affirmation, which gives way to anger again, which finally yields to self-affirmation. In fact, one of her songs is called "What Comes Around Goes Around."

STUDENT A: Well, if you're talking about the women's movement, a lot of women were angry about things that weren't fair or equal in society. Maybe Graves is referring to that anger in her songs?

STUDENT B: But don't forget, there's the affirming part too.

PROFESSOR: It's all a cycle. Ebbs and flows—like water—and always changing. Maybe starting angry, but turning into something positive. Notice how her voice reflects this: it's rough and filled with raw energy. You almost expect her voice to veer off into dissonance, be purposefully off-key, like a person shouting. But then she'll control her singing and always return to pitch. And that delicate guitar and percussion … how they support and contrast with her vocal moods. Her songs have the form of speak-singing at times.

STUDENT A: I don't know about speak-singing. Whenever I hear that term, I always feel the singer is, like, lecturing to the listener. I don't really think of that as entertainment.

PROFESSOR: Well, it may not be to everyone's taste. But just consider objectively what the singer is trying to accomplish with these songs. Graves maybe wants to simply tell you her experiences. Like the song "Alone and All One" calls out for solidarity, belonging to the world, even while accepting that this fast-food, high-tech, everyone's-busy-all-the-time world can be crazy. To become "all one," like she says, one must know what it is to be "alone."

STUDENT B: That's both ironic and true. Everybody wants to escape the craziness, but it's also important to reach out to someone who's lost.

PROFESSOR: Well, as she says, being open is "Not for Cowards"—the title of yet another song. In opening up to emotions, one affirms life. The experience becomes almost a ritual bathing in nature—and there you go, back to the water theme again.

On a personal note, I think one of Graves's lyrics especially captures the human condition: "There's only just a fine line/between alone and all one." That line's hard to see and hard to cross. But Graves seems to think that when both men and women find a common ground, they can come together to fill a need all people have. Wouldn't that outcome be worth throwing a tantrum for?

NARRATOR: Now use your notes to help you answer the questions.

What is the talk mainly about?

What can be inferred about the singer's attitude toward nature?

Listen to part of the talk again, and then answer the question.

PROFESSOR: She uses the water idea as a way to crash—not literally, of course— through such social constructs as fashion, gender, and the prim-and- proper way society thinks women should behave.

NARRATOR: Why does the professor say this:

PROFESSOR:	… not literally, of course …
NARRATOR:	Listen to part of the talk again, and then answer the question.
STUDENT A:	Well, if you're talking about the women's movement, a lot of women were angry about things that weren't fair or equal in society. Maybe Graves is referring to that anger in her songs?
STUDENT B:	But don't forget, there's the affirming part too. Narrator: What does the student mean when he says this: Student B: But don't forget, there's the affirming part too.
NARRATOR:	Listen to part of the talk again, and then answer the question.
PROFESSOR:	On a personal note, I think one of Graves's lyrics especially captures the human condition.
NARRATOR:	Why does the professor say this:
PROFESSOR:	On a personal note …
NARRATOR:	In the lecture, the professor discusses several themes covered in the songs. Indicate which of the following themes are considered by the singer.

Academic Talk 4: History

Track 32

NARRATOR:	Listen to part of a talk in a history class.
PROFESSOR:	By now, I hope you've all read Jefferson's book, Notes on the State of Virginia. Thomas Jefferson, uh, who most of you probably know as the third president of the United States, was a man of many talents. Musician, inventor, diplomat, writer. As you may recall, he wrote this book to answer questions posed to him by the French. They wanted to, to better understand the state of Virginia … Jefferson's home state. Now, he had quite a number of questions to answer, but he doesn't just answer them randomly. I hope you noted something of a structure to his material. We'll discuss this in greater depth later.
	First, though, I want to point out that by sorting out the questions into specific categories, Jefferson got the chance to write essays that would allow him to elaborate on many issues. He wasn't just going to focus on facts and figures on the state of Virginia. Instead, he was going to take the opportunity—articulate as he was—to find a platform for his philosophy and his knowledge. So, I'd like you to keep this question in mind as we look at these different essays, or, or chapters. Where does the objective scientist and writer begin … as Jefferson is asked to be? And where does a very subjective and opinionated human being come in? I'd like you to think about this … that both personas are reflected in his essays.
	So, uh, what does Jefferson do from the outset? Well, logically, he needs to introduce the place he wants to talk about. So in fact, he starts out by presenting a map of the state's topography, and brings his readers on a tour of the concrete elements of nature for about, oh, about the, the first half of the book.

According to the questions he's been given, he creates a logical succession of answers. First there's the land, then there's all the aspects of nature: rivers, mountains, mines, trees, animals, birds, people. He loads each discussion with as many "hard facts" as he can assemble from truly varied sources: established geographic measurements, documents and charters, personal calculations and astute personal observations, foreign and ancient sources, firsthand witnesses and practitioners, like uh, the miners themselves. And, Jefferson throws in some entertainment … anecdotes from Indian folklore and curious facts that a "tourist" would love to hear.

He also liked to create comparisons as a way of making a point. For example, he compares the Mississippi River with the Nile River! Now, everybody knew a good deal about the Nile in Jefferson's day, and so, because they were familiar with the nature of that ancient river, the French could transfer that understanding to a river they knew nothing about. Curiously, though, Jefferson is still selective, even though he has massive amounts of information to share. He just sort of sweeps over multitudes of facts with functional lists … lists of trees, lists of birds, whatever. Obviously, he didn't find it as important, for some reason, to describe leaves and birds in such minute detail as when he talked about the rivers and minerals. I'll leave you to figure out why he did that.

Speaking from his distinction as a key figure in the American fight for Independence … the writer of the Declaration of Independence, as I hope you all recall … you'll see that Jefferson saves the best stuff for last. By laying out the land of Virginia—that is physically … the land and its nature—he now moves into discussing the larger and more conceptual issues that make up the state. Notice a big difference. He begins to talk more forcefully in the "I" voice. It's, it's almost as if his own life, now, becomes a source of knowledge. He's an authority on politics, economics, trade, human relations, government, history. And now he speaks in broader terms, in powerful rhetoric. Here's our chance for deeper discussion the next time we meet. What's Jefferson accomplished by doing this? His shift in voice is significant, even though his style seems to clash with the first half of the book. Let's look at specific sections now, to see if we can understand Jefferson's ulterior motives behind these notes.

NARRATOR: Now use your notes to help you answer the questions.

What is the talk mainly about?

What is the logical progression of Jefferson's description of Virginia?

How do the two parts of Jefferson's book reflect his personality?

Listen to part of the talk again, and then answer the question.

PROFESSOR: Curiously, though, Jefferson is still selective, even though he has massive amounts of information to share. He just sort of sweeps over multitudes of facts with functional lists …

NARRATOR: What does the professor mean when he says this:

PROFESSOR:	He just sort of sweeps over multitudes of facts …
NARRATOR:	Listen to part of the talk again, and then answer the question.
PROFESSOR:	Obviously, he didn't find it as important, for some reason, to describe leaves and birds in such minute detail as when he talked about the rivers and minerals. I'll leave you to figure out why he did that.
NARRATOR:	Why does the professor say this:
PROFESSOR:	I'll leave you to figure out …
NARRATOR:	Listen to part of the talk again, and then answer the question.
PROFESSOR:	… you'll see that Jefferson saves the best stuff for last. By laying out the land of Virginia—that is physically … the land and its nature—he now moves into discussing the larger and more conceptual issues that make up the state.
NARRATOR:	What does the professor imply when he says this:
PROFESSOR:	… Jefferson saves the best stuff for last.

SPEAKING SECTION

Task 1

Track 33

NARRATOR: Task One. Talk about a challenge that you've had to face and explain how you managed to overcome it. Include details and examples in your response.

Task 2

Track 34

NARRATOR: Task Two. Some people want to be friends with their parents. Others prefer to maintain the more traditional parent-child relationship. Which approach do you favor and why? Give details and examples to support your choice.

Task 3

Track 35

NARRATOR: Task Three. Listen to two students as they discuss the announcement.

STUDENT A: Why is it that the athletes always get all the money? It's so unfair!

STUDENT B: Have you seen the swimming pool we have now? Can you believe we've had the same pool since 1904?

STUDENT A: And can you believe I live in the only dorm on campus that doesn't have Internet access? And that the bio labs haven't been renovated since my dad was a student here? I have nothing against sports. I'm only saying that the university should spend its limited resources in ways that'll do the most good for the largest number of people.

STUDENT B: Athletics are important. They help students relieve stress and keep their bodies in good shape. And our sports teams help foster school spirit.

STUDENT A: That's all very nice, but I just think the administration has its priorities all wrong. They should put academics first. Talk about stress! I could use a new language lab to improve my grades. That'd help my stress.

STUDENT B: Look at the bright side. Maybe our fancy new sports center will earn so much money in ticket sales that they'll be able to add several labs.

NARRATOR: Now get ready to answer the question.

NARRATOR: The man expresses his opinion about the announcement made by the alumni office. State his opinion and explain the reasons he gives for holding that opinion.

Task 4

Track 36

NARRATOR:	Task Four. Now listen to part of a talk in a zoology class.
PROFESSOR:	People who lived near Yellowstone raised a lot of fuss when wolves were returned there by scientists in the mid-'90s. The old prejudices and fears came right to the surface again. The "big bad wolf" coming to get you. It's a lot of nonsense really, and the Yellowstone Wolf Project has helped prove that. The wolves are not a problem—in fact, a lack of wolves, or an absence of wolves is the problem. How many of you have heard of someone being attacked by a wolf? No one, right? Now how many of you know someone who got into a car accident because deer were on the roads or highways? Or have neighbors who can't grow flowers or vegetables because the deer eat everything? Yeah, a lot more of you. We have a serious deer problem in this country because we have no predators to control the deer population. The deer numbers are out of control, but we have people worried about a couple of dozen wolves in Yellowstone. Well, the wolves haven't been causing problems to the neighbors of Yellowstone. Cattle and sheep and horses simply aren't being attacked. The wolves have plenty of deer in the park to keep them busy. We need more wolves—not less.
NARRATOR:	Now get ready to answer the question.
NARRATOR:	The professor talks about the results of wolves being brought back to Yellowstone National Park. Explain what those results are and how those results are contrary to what people living near the park expected.

Task 5

Track 37

NARRATOR:	Task Five. Listen to a dialogue between two students. Student A (male): Hey, Eileen. You busy? I could use some advice. Student B (female): What's going on, Henry?
STUDENT A:	I'm thinking of dropping Chinese and going back to taking French …
STUDENT B:	Dropping Chinese? But I thought you loved the class!
STUDENT A:	Oh, I do. It's a great language! It's just that it's so time-consuming. And I always feel like I have to choose between studying Chinese and studying for my other classes. My grades are starting to slip.
STUDENT B:	It just seems like such a shame for you to dump Chinese now. You've already taken two semesters. You've put in so much time and effort. Couldn't you drop one of your other classes, one of your electives, to leave you more time to study?
STUDENT A:	I guess … Maybe … But I'd hoped to get good enough to use Chinese professionally. I just don't think that's ever gonna happen.
STUDENT B:	Don't sell yourself short. Your French is pretty good, isn't it?

STUDENT A:	That's just it. I'm already pretty advanced. With a little effort, I could probably become pretty fluent. I can't imagine ever becoming fluent in Chinese. It's too hard.
STUDENT B:	Have you ever thought of taking one of those intensive summer courses? Maybe even studying abroad?
STUDENT A:	I'd love to study abroad—especially in China—but I could never afford it. Even with a partial scholarship, I'm having trouble making ends meet.
STUDENT B:	My friend, Anne, studied abroad last term and she was able to apply her financial aid to her study abroad program. The study abroad office is hosting an information session next week. Go check it out.
STUDENT A:	I don't know … That seems like a lot of commitment to make to a language I may never excel in. Maybe I'll look into where I can use French professionally.
NARRATOR:	Now get ready to answer the question.
NARRATOR:	The students discuss two solutions to the man's problem. Describe the problem. Then state which of the two solutions you prefer and why.

Task 6

Track 38

NARRATOR:	Task Six. For this task, you will hear a short academic talk. You will hear a question about it. You will then have 20 seconds to prepare your response and 60 seconds to speak.
	Listen to part of a talk in an American government class.
PROFESSOR:	In the 1960s, the United States Supreme Court handed down a landmark decision that affirmed the legal rights of persons accused of a crime. Gideon v. Wainwright centered on a man named Clarence Gideon, who was arrested for breaking into a bar in 1961. When Gideon asked the court to appoint a lawyer to defend him, the court denied his request, saying that state law required the court to provide defendants with an attorney only in capital cases, that is to say, cases involving a person's death or the death penalty. As Gideon was too poor to afford a lawyer, he defended himself at his trial and—perhaps not surprisingly— was sentenced to jail. While he was in prison, Gideon studied law books on his own and eventually wrote a petition asking the Supreme Court to hear his case. In its decision the Supreme Court ruled that Gideon's right to a fair trial—guaranteed under the Fourth Amendment to the Constitution—had been violated. The Supreme Court ruled that every state must provide a lawyer for any person who's accused of a crime and cannot afford to pay for his or her own legal defense. Gideon was given a second trial. This time, he was represented by a defense attorney and he was declared innocent.
	You might be asking yourself why the Fourth Amendment was relevant to Gideon's case. In considering the case, the Supreme Court focused

on what exactly is meant by "a fair trial." And what the Supreme Court decided was that forcing a man with no legal expertise to defend himself in court, simply because he did not have the means to pay for a lawyer, put the defendant at an unfair disadvantage.

NARRATOR: Now get ready to answer the question.

NARRATOR: Using points and examples from the talk, explain why Gideon's case was important and what values are reflected in the Supreme Court's decision.

WRITING SECTION

Task 1

Track 39

NARRATOR: Listen to part of a talk on the topic you just read about.

PROFESSOR: Like many other historical episodes, nobody is really quite sure what happened to the battleship Maine in Havana Harbor on February 15th, 1898. The ship was destroyed by a blast that killed 260 of the 350 soldiers aboard, but the cause of the blast is still uncertain. The reaction of the American media and public is somewhat influential in what happened next, but the ensuing war between the U.S. and Spain was not solely caused by "yellow journalism," as some might suggest.

One thing to consider is why the Maine was in the harbor in the first place. The U.S. government claimed that it was a friendly visit, but the had long been interested in increasing American influence in Cuba. While there are some people who blame the media for causing the war, the reality of the situation is that U.S. actions prior to the explosion show that the United States had been preparing for war long before the battleship sank. American politicians were outwardly concerned about having a strong European presence so close to our own shores. The long American tradition of anticolonialism factored into our support of Cuba, as did a fear of the destruction of our own economic interests in Cuba and a potential trade threat to the U.S. in the Caribbean.

While Pulitzer and Hearst definitely succeeded in stirring up some public resentment against Spain, the facts show that the U.S. had been bracing for a war with the superpower far before the newspapers printed their sensationalized account of the ship's sinking. The press can influence people in subtle and overt ways, but the war with Spain would have come about, regardless of how it was represented in New York's newspapers.

NARRATOR: Summarize the points made in the talk you just heard, explaining how they cast doubt on the points made in the reading.

PRACTICE TEST 4

LISTENING SECTION

Dialogue 1

Track 40

NARRATOR:	Listen to a dialogue between a student and a professor.
PROFESSOR:	Oh, Jerry, come in. My office hours have just started.
STUDENT:	Hi, Professor Wright. I, uh, needed to clarify something on the project you gave out yesterday. You said it, uh, the project, should have five parts, but I only see one here.
PROFESSOR:	Yes, I mentioned in class I'd be giving out the other parts as we go along because I, I want you to just develop one part at a time.
STUDENT:	I don't remember that—oh, I came in late.
PROFESSOR:	Yes, right, you were about 15 minutes late.
STUDENT:	I'm really sorry. I got stuck at work, then I got stuck in traffic, and then I got stuck trying to park! When it rains, it pours.
PROFESSOR:	I marked you down as present when I saw you. But if that happens again, please come to me after class and let me know. It's a big class, and if you're just slipping in and out, I might mark you absent when you aren't.
STUDENT:	Thanks.
PROFESSOR:	Now, did you have questions on the part I handed out?
STUDENT:	To be honest, I haven't gone over it since class. We're supposed to describe the school we're teaching in, right?
PROFESSOR:	The school, the students, the demographics. Anything to help me understand where you're student teaching.
STUDENT:	Okay. Uh, what's coming up in the other parts?
PROFESSOR:	Well, I explain that in the handout too. But basically, for the second part, I want you to describe a topic you'll be teaching this semester to your students. You're teaching math, right?
STUDENT:	No, I teach Spanish.
PROFESSOR:	Oh, okay. So then pick a topic in Spanish, like, um, teaching a particular verb, and tell me how you'd carry out that lesson.
STUDENT:	Oh, I can do like going to the park and teach the verb *play* or *run* in different tenses.
PROFESSOR:	That's right, and you could delve into, maybe popular sports in Spain—some aspect of the culture. I want details about how you'd carry that out in the classroom.
STUDENT:	And the other parts?

PROFESSOR:	I expect you to write test questions for the students, as well as how you'd evaluate their quest—I mean their answers. That's parts three and four. And in part five, I want you to write a reflection paper.
STUDENT:	Like what I learned?
PROFESSOR:	And how you could improve what you did, things like that.
STUDENT:	That's a lot of work. But if I'm going to be a teacher someday, this is how I learn.
PROFESSOR:	That's the point, Jerry.
NARRATOR:	Now use your notes to help you answer the questions.
	What is the focus of the professor's class project?
	Why did the student need to talk with the professor?
	What subject does the student teach?
	Listen to part of the dialogue again, and then answer the question.
PROFESSOR:	I marked you down as present when I saw you. But if that happens again, please come to me after class and let me know. It's a big class, and if you're just slipping in and out, I might mark you absent when you aren't.
NARRATOR:	What is the professor implying?
	Listen to part of the dialogue again, and then answer the question.
STUDENT:	I'm really sorry. I got stuck at work, then I got stuck in traffic, and then I got stuck trying to park! When it rains, it pours.
NARRATOR:	What can be inferred about the student?

Dialogue 2

Track 41

NARRATOR:	Listen to a dialogue between a student and an administrator.
STUDENT:	Hi, I got this letter saying there's a problem with my activity fees?
ADMINISTRATOR:	Umm ... Oh yes, we thought it'd be easier to clear everything up if you came in. We don't seem to have received your activity fees payment. I know there's never been a problem before, but ... umm, I'm afraid it's university policy that we have to receive the first installment of fees before the semester starts. The fees are normally deposited by wire transfer into the university's account, aren't they?
STUDENT:	That's right, my dad wires the money from Taiwan. I've got a copy of the wire instructions here. It's in both Chinese and English.
ADMINISTRATOR:	Excellent. Let me just check this against our records. Well ... this all seems okay ... No, look ... two digits of our account number have been reversed.
STUDENT:	So does that mean the money's gone to someone else's account?
ADMINISTRATOR:	Well, that's possible. Or the other account number might not actually exist. Then the bank would try to find the account where

	it's supposed to go and if that's not possible, they'd send it back … though that could take some time … possibly a few weeks.
STUDENT:	Well, my dad didn't say anything about the money being returned. But I can ask him to check it out with the bank back home.
ADMINISTRATOR:	Right. In the meantime though, as I said, it's actually university policy that fees need to be paid before the semester starts on Monday. Would you be able to … um … ?
STUDENT:	Wow, that's a lot of money. I don't have that. I mean, I'd need to wait till my dad could wire it, which wouldn't really be any faster, would it?
ADMINISTRATOR:	No, that's true. Okay … well, your fees have always been paid on time up to now and we do have evidence that the funds were actually sent. I think I'd better take a copy of this, if you don't mind … Okay, I'll need to get this confirmed by my manager … She'll be in Monday … but I don't think there'll be a problem extending the payment deadline by, say, two weeks. That should give your dad time to sort out the payment error and make a new payment. Is there a phone number where we can reach you on Monday in case my manager needs to ask you more questions?
STUDENT:	Yes, I'll be at 555-6789 most of the day. I do hope this gets sorted out quickly. And thanks for being so understanding.
NARRATOR:	Now use your notes to help you answer the questions.
	Why does the student go to the administrative office?
	What has happened with the bank transfer?
	Listen to part of the dialogue again, and then answer the question.
ADMINISTRATOR:	… as I said, it's actually university policy that fees need to be paid before the semester starts on Monday. Would you be able to … um … ?
NARRATOR:	What does the administrator mean when he says this:
ADMINISTRATOR:	Would you be able to … um … ?
NARRATOR:	What does the administrator offer to do?
	What will the administrator probably do?

Academic Talk 1: Film Studies

Track 42

NARRATOR:	Listen to a part of a talk in a film studies class.
PROFESSOR:	We take so much for granted when we see comedy films today. We forget that films have their roots in a time at the beginning of the 20th century when no one on film spoke in real voices, and when all comedy relied on the visual rather than the verbal. One of the great icons of silent film comedy was Buster Keaton, and we'll be seeing some of his films over the next couple of weeks.
STUDENT A:	But I thought Charlie Chaplin was the only major comedian back then—or, uh, icon, did you say? Wasn't he better than Keaton?

STUDENT B:	No way! I've seen both, but I think Keaton's much more interesting. He's like … less in your face than Chaplin.
PROFESSOR:	Now that's an interesting way to put it! Yes, Chaplin was a very defined character, with his tramp outfit, derby, cane, and little mustache. Chaplin was considered the international king of comedy. His comedy often dealt with some very emotionally poignant stories that focused on poverty, immigration, and social injustice. Keaton was more cerebral, if you will. He wasn't highly emotional … or was he?
STUDENT A:	How can you be emotional and cerebral at the same time?
STUDENT B:	Ted, just because someone might look at life philosophically, let's say, doesn't mean they don't have deep feelings about their ideas.
PROFESSOR:	I'd agree with that. Maybe Keaton showed a different, more subtle kind of emotion. He wasn't, as you said, in your face. We can definitely pick up that point again once we've looked at a few of his short films. Now, in keeping with this kind of subtlety, or maybe a mask even, Keaton's most famous trademark was his deadpan face … he never cracked a smile. It was almost like he was unable to smile—and there weren't other actors around trying comedy with an unsmiling face like that. And, uh, what else? Oh right, he wore a flat porkpie hat, which rarely flew off, even when he was doing incredible physical feats like somersaults, spins, twists, and pratfalls. Very subtle slapstick, that hat. And though his face was pale and unchanging, if you look deeply into his eyes, you may very well see all the expressions you need to know to, to understand how Keaton views his world and reacts to it.
STUDENT B:	And I read somewhere that Keaton was much more interested in the camera, like how it worked, than Chaplin. Like, how he could shot, I mean, shoot more visually interesting shots for comedy purposes.
PROFESSOR:	Well, you're moving us right along here! Definitely. Although Chaplin directed many of his own films, Keaton … as a director himself … was even more interested in the power and flexibility of the camera. He'd use the camera as a tool to build his humor, to be part of the joke. In one scene—which we'll see today—from his short film called One Week, … Keaton pans his camera from side to side to reveal the punch line of his visual joke. The comedian doesn't give the punch line, as you might expect, instead the camera does. It's a good example of a comedian who's not only created a funny situation, but knows how to use all the elements within the frame to milk the humor in that situation. Keep that in mind as you watch the film. Okay, uh, yes, Ted?
STUDENT A:	And I think Chaplin had more experience in show business than Keaton did, though, didn't he?
PROFESSOR:	Believe it or not, Keaton was actually a vaudeville star from the time he was nine months old. According to some stories, Buster crawled onto the stage while his father—also an actor—was performing a monologue.

Apparently, the audience loved the baby more than the father, but his father knew a good thing when he saw it. So he added his son to the family act, and that was the start of a stage career that lasted until 1917, when Keaton the adult entered the world of silent film comedy.

STUDENT B: Was that in Hollywood?

PROFESSOR: Actually, Keaton got his start in New York. He visited a studio on a whim and met another comedian who'd become a great friend and influence his life forever … Roscoe "Fatty" Arbuckle. Right on the spot, Arbuckle gave Keaton his first chance to appear in a comedy short called The Butcher Boy, where he does some great comic business, fighting with molasses and flour. You can imagine the mess that happens when comedians start playing with props like that. Even as he was working on that short film, Keaton began to investigate how the camera worked and how he could use it as a tool to develop his brand of comedy. And the rest, as we say, is history.

NARRATOR: Now use your notes to help you answer the questions.

What is the talk mainly about?

What does the professor say is interesting about Keaton?

What can be inferred about Keaton's approach to filmmaking?

Listen to part of the talk again, and then answer the question.

STUDENT B: And I read somewhere that Keaton was much more interested in the camera, like how it worked, than Chaplin. Like, how he could shot, I mean, shoot more visually interesting shots for comedy purposes.

PROFESSOR: Well, you're moving us right along here! Definitely.

NARRATOR: Why does the professor say this:

PROFESSOR: Well, you're moving us right along here!

NARRATOR: Listen to part of the talk again, and then answer the question.

PROFESSOR: It's a good example of a comedian who's not only created a funny situation, but knows how to use all the elements within the frame to milk the humor in that situation.

NARRATOR: What does the professor mean when she says:

PROFESSOR: … but knows how to use all the elements within the frame to milk the humor in that situation.

NARRATOR: According to the talk, which of the following are events from Buster Keaton's life that helped shape his career?

Academic Talk 2: Biology

Track 43

NARRATOR: Listen to part of a talk in a biology class.

PROFESSOR: All right, today's topic is diabetes. Diabetes is a disease marked by high levels of glucose in the blood. Now, can some- one tell me what blood glucose is?

STUDENT A: It's blood sugar, right?

PROFESSOR: Yes, the cells of our bodies use blood glucose, blood sugar, as a source of energy. However, before our bodies can use this blood glucose, it must move from the bloodstream into our individual cells. And this process requires a protein called insulin, which is produced by the pancreas. Insulin helps blood glucose move from the bloodstream into individual cells, so your body can use it for energy. Questions … ? Okay, so what is diabetes? Diabetes occurs when the body doesn't produce enough insulin or when the body is unable to use insulin properly. With low insulin levels, it becomes very difficult for your body to use blood glucose for energy. And when the body cannot convert blood glucose into energy, what does it do? Any ideas … ? Okay, it begins to break down stored fat to use for fuel. And this can cause problems because using too much fat for fuel can lead to high blood pressure, and strokes. So high blood sugar really is a killer—

STUDENT B: Excuse me, um … how exactly does high blood sugar damage you?

PROFESSOR: Lots of ways. First, your kidneys. Your kidneys remove impurities from the blood—that's their job. When you have extra glucose in the blood, this glucose passes through the kidneys, but the kidneys can't get rid of it all. Since not all of the extra glucose is removed by the kidneys, this excess glucose—accompanied by water—spills into the urine. The body tries to get rid of this glucose and water mix and this causes frequent urination, excessive thirst, and hunger. If diabetes isn't treated, it can cause further complications, including kidney failure … and there are other things, like blindness, and heart disease. Now presently, there is no cure for diabetes, but—yes, Margaret?

STUDENT A: But they say that foods with high sugar contents can cause diabetes. So, so wouldn't cutting down on sweets help get rid of diabetes?

PROFESSOR: Actually, that's a myth. Diabetes is caused by a combination of genetic and environmental factors. Sweets are no more out of bounds to people with diabetes than they are to the rest of us, especially if they are eaten as part of a healthy diet and exercise plan. On top of that, people who take insulin to treat their diabetes may sometimes need to eat high-sugar foods to prevent their blood glucose levels from falling too low. Now as I was saying, there is no cure for diabetes. So a person with diabetes must control the amount of glucose in their blood through regular physical exercise, a carefully controlled diet, and medication. They may require insulin injections a few times a day, to provide the body with the insulin it doesn't produce.

And this can be tricky! You see, our bodies don't require a *constant* amount of insulin, the amount we need actually *varies*. So diabetics typically have to measure the level of glucose in a drop of their blood several times each day. If the blood glucose level is too high or too low, they can adjust the amount of insulin injected, as well as the amount of physical exercise they do, or their food intake to maintain a normal blood glucose level.

STUDENT B:	What happens if a person with diabetes injects too much insulin?
PROFESSOR:	If a person with diabetes injects too much insulin, it can produce low blood sugar levels. This can lead to hypoglycemia, a condition characterized by shakiness, confusion, and anxiety.
STUDENT B:	So low insulin levels mean blood sugar levels get too high, but overly high insulin levels means your blood sugar level drops too low.
PROFESSOR:	That's right. You want insulin levels that are neither too high, nor too low.
STUDENT A:	So let's say a diabetic injects too much insulin, and now they drop to where their blood sugar is too low. What should they do?
STUDENT B:	You said it earlier: they should eat sweets … try to boost their blood sugar levels, right?
PROFESSOR:	Yes, by consuming foods with sugar, such as fruit juice or sugar candy, many diabetics can eliminate hypoglycemic symptoms.
	Okay, so to recap, even today, scientists are unsure of the exact cause of diabetes. It continues to be a mystery, although both genetics and environmental factors such as obesity and the lack of exercise appear to play roles. But the basic steps all diabetics have to follow are the same: eat right, manage your weight, stay physically active, stop smoking, and take the diabetes medicines if prescribed by your doctor.
NARRATOR:	Now use your notes to help you answer the questions.
	What is the discussion mainly about?
	Which of the following facts about diabetes does the professor mention?
	Listen to part of the talk again, and then answer the question.
PROFESSOR:	Now presently, there is no cure for diabetes, but—yes, Margaret?
STUDENT A:	But they say that foods with high sugar contents can cause diabetes. So, so wouldn't cutting down on sweets help get rid of diabetes?
NARRATOR:	What does the student suggest?
	Listen to part of the talk again, and then answer the question.
PROFESSOR:	Diabetes is caused by a combination of genetic and environmental factors. Sweets are no more out of bounds to people with diabetes than they are to the rest of us, especially if they are eaten as part of a healthy diet and exercise plan.
NARRATOR:	What does the professor mean when he says this:
PROFESSOR:	Sweets are no more out of bounds to people with diabetes than they are to the rest of us …
NARRATOR:	Listen to part of the talk again, and then answer the question.
PROFESSOR:	Now as I was saying, there is no cure for diabetes. So a person with diabetes must control the amount of glucose in their blood through regular physical exercise, a carefully controlled diet, and medication.
NARRATOR:	What is the purpose of the professor's comment?
	Which of the following are diabetics required to do regularly?

Academic Talk 3: Film Studies

Track 44

NARRATOR:	Listen to part of a discussion in an American Studies class.
PROFESSOR:	Does anyone know the old saying, "One action can speak a thousand words"? Well, keep this proverb in mind as we consider our topic today. How a book gets adapted into a movie. Today, I'll be referring to Tom Wolfe's gigantic book—over 700 pages—called Bonfire of the Vanities. It was turned into a, oh, roughly two-hour movie of the same name by director Brian De Palma.
	Imagine sitting down to the task of reading lots of descriptive detail, more characters than you can shake a stick at, and numerous twists and turns in the plot, and digging out only the essence that you should include in a film—a totally different medium—to get the author's point across, capture the quality of the book, and yet create a completely different work of art. A filmmaker's work of art, compared with the author's work of art.
STUDENT A:	It seems to me that it's too hard to make the structures of each art form mesh.
STUDENT B:	Yeah, but it happens all the time. Books are always being adapted into movies.
STUDENT A:	Well, maybe it happens all the time, but it doesn't always work out. Lots of movies fall really short of the book.
PROFESSOR:	Yes, we'll need to address that issue. Of course, a novel follows structures that distinguish it from other literary forms, like a short story, a poem, or a play. So too a film based on a novel must draw upon its own defining cinematic structures and techniques to convey story, emotion, and message. Skilled novelists rely on the energy of the printed word to create an intimate bond with the reader. In a film, the printed word rarely factors in.
STUDENT A:	Film's purely visual and audio. So the novel has to be re-created through a lot of things that the book doesn't even worry about. Image, sound, music, and action.
STUDENT B:	Yeah, and the book has the leisure to describe all that in hundreds of words, while the film has to get its point across quickly in a limited number of shots.
PROFESSOR:	That's the dilemma. It's hard to make a worthy film adaptation for an audience who knows the book. One criticism about the Bonfire film was that it digressed from the novel in significant ways instead of remaining faithful to the book's satiric humor, rich detail, and linear development. Don't worry, we'll go through the film and examine key sequences to see what I mean. I'm just giving you a thumbnail sketch of what to keep in mind.
	But I'll describe one example right now from the opening before we see anything. The book and the film both wanted to convey the hypocrisy

and tension that society creates. Wolfe starts out with a chaotic scene describing the mayor and included a lot of punctuation—exclamation points, dashes, ellipses—and wordplay, all very verbal mechanisms. It's all intended to show the mayor getting hit on the head with a mayonnaise jar … remember that from the book? Well, De Palma opens his film with a newspaper reporter about to receive an award for his book. But, the reporter doesn't even appear in the book until much later. What is De Palma doing?

STUDENT A: I guess he's forcing us to see the story through the reporter's eyes instead of just an objective set of eyes looking at life in general.

STUDENT B: That's a radical choice, isn't it? I mean, I'd think he would have to ask himself if that's what the author really wanted.

PROFESSOR: Of course. And as the audience, you'd have to ask yourself, was that an effective choice? And, of course, always ask my favorite question: why or why not? Those who adapt books into films have to take liberties sometimes, but are those liberties in the best interest of the book? Characters are dropped, new ones are added. Dialogue is omitted or rewritten. All the details that a novelist luxuriates in might go out the window. Tough choices.

STUDENT A: Like, somehow I always feel like I'm missing something from a film adaptation. I'm expecting a lot more after I've read the book. I think I'd prefer to read the book after the movie to see what I missed.

PROFESSOR: That's why lots of times, audiences do leave the film adaptation … disappointed. It's hard to separate the film from the book, especially when the book really grabbed you. And that reminds me of another saying you've all probably heard or used: "Don't bother going to the movie. Read the book instead." Right? Okay, let's begin to examine why a film adaptation, which should capture the book, would motivate someone to say that.

NARRATOR: Now use your notes to help you answer the questions.

What is the talk mainly about?

Why does the professor mention the first scene in the film?

According to the talk, which can be inferred about film adaptations?

Listen to part of the talk again, and then answer the question.

PROFESSOR: Does anyone know the old saying, "One action can speak a thousand words"? Well, keep this proverb in mind as we consider our topic today.

NARRATOR: Why does the professor say this:

PROFESSOR: … "One action can speak a thousand words"?

NARRATOR: Listen to part of the talk again, and then answer the question.

STUDENT A: It seems to me that it's too hard to make the structures of each art form mesh.

STUDENT B: Yeah, but it happens all the time. Books are always being adapted into movies.

STUDENT A:	Well, maybe it happens all the time, but it doesn't always work out. Lots of movies fall really short of the book.
NARRATOR:	What does the student mean by this:
STUDENT	Lots of movies fall really short of the book.
NARRATOR:	In the talk, the professor describes a number of things that can be affected by an adaptation. Choose three of the answer choices below that were mentioned in the talk.

Academic Talk 4: Astronomy

Track 45

NARRATOR:	Listen to part of a talk in an astronomy class.
PROFESSOR:	Today we're going to talk about the planet Mercury. Okay … it's not easy to see Mercury—it's so close to the sun that it's only visible during, uh … around dawn and dusk, never in darkness. It's also close to the horizon when it is visible to the naked eye, so we're seeing it through the maximum thickness of the atmosphere. When it's higher in the sky, it can be seen through telescopes, but you can't actually make out any, any detail, since there's no real contrast against the bright daytime sky.
	So far we've only sent one probe to Mercury, um … that was in 1963, oh, sorry, I meant 1973. So the first probe went up in '73 and *Mariner 10* flew by the planet three times in 1974 and '75 and sent back a lot of information. A lot of that information was in the form of pictures of about half of Mercury's surface. Because Mercury's so close to the sun, it's really hard to get *to* Mercury and even harder to put a probe in orbit around it. That's because of the sun's tremendous gravitational field. Recently though, a new form of propulsion … called an ion engine, has opened up new possibilities for exploring Mercury. It'll make a probe less dependent on picking up thrust from other planets to counteract the gravitational pull of the sun, as is currently necessary with conventional rockets.
	Two missions to Mercury are actually being planned right now. NASA is sending a probe called *Messenger*, planned to arrive in 2008, for three flybys, and will enter Mercury's orbit in 2011.
	The European Space Agency is sending a larger mission known as BepiColombo. This mission will have three spacecraft, including a landing module and a module designed to investigate the magnetic field. It's planned for launch in 2008 or '9, so about the same time NASA's mission reaches Mercury.
	One interesting thing is that the *Mariner*'s pictures of Mercury, about 1,800 in total, all show only one side of the planet. Of course this is because the planet rotates very slowly … about once every 58 and a half Earth days. Radar pictures taken from the earth suggest that the other side of Mercury has large mountains. There may, um … be volcanoes, though it's unlikely that they're still active.

Scientists are hoping to get answers to several unsolved mysteries with the *Messenger* and BepiColombo missions. One is why Mercury is so dense ... over 70 percent iron, twice as much as the other inner planets ... Venus, Earth, the moon, and Mars. Maybe when the planets were formed, there was more dense material like iron close to the sun, or maybe Mercury was originally a much larger planet whose surface was blasted off into space leaving the iron core, or maybe the heat from the sun in the early days of the solar system boiled away the lighter elements from the planet's surface.

Spectrometers carried by the probes should be able to tell us which, if any, of these three theories is correct, depending on what elements they find. If Mercury's composition is similar to the moon, it's unlikely that heavy elements were concentrated near the sun. If Mercury's surface was blasted away, elements like aluminum would float to the surface and solidify, confirming the second theory. Finally, the absence of lighter, volatile elements like sodium on the surface might confirm the third theory ... that Mercury has had part of its surface evaporated away by the sun's heat.

Hopefully the probes may also tell us something about Mercury's um ... magnetic field. The Earth's magnetic field protects us from dangerous radiation from the sun. Venus and Mars have hardly any magnetic field, but Mercury has one, and we're not quite sure how. We guess it's generated in the iron core, but because Mercury has no atmosphere to speak of, and so no, ... no ionosphere to complete the circuit, and allow the magnetic field to be sustained like it is here on Earth, it's a bit of a mystery.

One last thing that the BepiColombo mission will test has to do with Einstein's general theory of relativity. Mercury has quite an elliptical orbit, which Einstein explained in terms of a curvature of the time-space continuum close to the sun. The BepiColombo probe will be traveling through the presumed curvature, so the readings on its instruments will provide a powerful test of Einstein's predictions.

NARRATOR: Now use your notes to help you answer the questions.

What is the main topic of this talk?

Why does the professor begin by discussing how difficult it is to see Mercury from Earth?

What can be inferred about Mercury?

Why are the *Mariner 10* pictures all of one side of Mercury?

What will spectrometry determine about Mercury?

What is true of Mercury's magnetic field?

SPEAKING SECTION

Task 1

Track 46

NARRATOR:	Task one. Describe a movie you've recently watched and explain why you liked it. Include details and examples to support your explanation.

Task 2

Track 47

NARRATOR:	Task two. Some people think that television, the Internet, and other electronic media make the printed book obsolete as a source of information or entertainment. Other people say that printed books will continue to play an important role in society. Which view do you agree with? Include details and examples in your explanation.

Task 3

Track 48

NARRATOR:	Task three. Now listen to two students as they discuss the announcement.
STUDENT A:	You should apply, Sarah.
STUDENT B:	Me? No way! I'm swamped as it is. I couldn't possibly take on something like this. I actually know the person who did it last year. That position's a lot of work.
STUDENT A:	It doesn't have to be. Remember that leadership skills seminar we took last semester? Rule number one: A great leader is someone who knows how to delegate. The trick is to find other people to do all the work and then make sure they get the job done.
STUDENT B:	Look, it's not that I don't want to do it. I'm sure it would have its benefits, but I really need to concentrate on looking for a job. Graduation's right around the corner and I haven't even gotten a résumé together.
STUDENT A:	Yeah, but just think how good that position would look on your résumé. And the club would be a great way to make connections. You'd meet lots of local business leaders, socialize with them. Next thing you know, they ask you to come by the office for an interview …
STUDENT B:	No wonder you want to go into sales.
NARRATOR:	Now get ready to answer the question.
NARRATOR:	The man tries to persuade the woman to do something. Say what he tries to persuade her to do and explain the reasons he gives.

Task 4

Track 49

NARRATOR: Task four. Now listen to part of a talk in a computer science class.

PROFESSOR: A very real—and growing—problem that most, if not all of you will face if you continue in the technology field, is hacking. Some of you might wish otherwise, but simply put, hacking is a felony in the United States and most other countries. Now, when it's done by request and under a contract between an ethical hacker and an organization, it's okay. But that's not really what we're talking about when we're talking about hacking. Hacking is entering a person's or organization's computer without permission. This is unethical and a serious crime. No matter what your reasons are, how you might claim to be serving a higher good, it's really the same thing as breaking into someone's office or home. That's a crime. Everyone knows that. What baffles me is that in this day and age people still are trying to create a distinction between entering some- one's home and entering someone's computer. If they haven't asked you to do it, you're in the wrong. Period. End of discussion. Even the so-called "joyriders" are in the wrong. Those are the hackers who say they're just rising to the challenge of breaking into a company's supposedly secure system, only to leave without doing anything or causing any harm. If you break into this computer lab, do you think the police wouldn't arrest you just because you didn't take anything?

NARRATOR: Now get ready to answer the question.

NARRATOR: Two opinions on computer hacking are given in the reading. Explain which of these views the professor holds and how she supports her opinion.

Task 5

Track 50

NARRATOR: Task five. Now listen to a conversation between two students. Student A (male): Nadine, you gotta minute? I could use some advice. Student B (female): What's the trouble, Sean?

STUDENT A: I'm thinking of switching advisors …

STUDENT B: I don't get it. You were so excited when Dr. Henderson was assigned to be your advisor. Isn't he some kind of big shot?

STUDENT A: Yeah, he won a big chem prize a couple of years ago and they say he has a good chance to win a Nobel Prize in the next couple of years.

STUDENT B: So, your advisor's a genius. You should be happy.

STUDENT A: I am, I guess. It's just that … well … I never get to see him. He's never around. He's always off attending some international conference. His assistant gave the last two lectures.

STUDENT B: Ah, the "Case of the Missing Professor."

STUDENT A:	So I'm thinking of switching to another advisor, one I can have more contact with. But I can't decide.
STUDENT B:	A recommendation letter from Henderson would sure help you get into grad school. But he's not gonna recommend you if he doesn't get to know you first. Why don't you write to him? Tell him you're really interested in his research. Ask if you could help out in his lab in some way. I'm sure he'd welcome an eager helper.
STUDENT A:	You think? I'm just a sophomore. I'm thinking I should find another professor in the department who'd take me under his wing, and maybe even help me, you know, make contacts in the field. In the end, that might be a lot more useful.
STUDENT B:	I think you're selling yourself short. Show some initiative and make yourself known to him. High-profile people like him respect go-getters. Even if you don't learn anything from him directly, his endorsement could open a lot of doors for you.
STUDENT A:	Yeah, but I'd sure like to get some feedback and learn some- thing from my advisor too. It shouldn't all be politics.
NARRATOR:	Now get ready to answer the question.
NARRATOR:	The students discuss two possible solutions to the man's problem. Describe the problem. Then state which solution you prefer and explain why.

Task 6

Track 51

NARRATOR:	Task six. Now listen to part of a talk in an urban history class.
PROFESSOR:	The written history of what is today New York City traces its roots to 1626, when a group of colonists arrived from the Netherlands to establish a settlement they called New Amsterdam. The story of how the Dutch purchased the island of Manhattan from the Indians for the equivalent of $24 is legendary. But beyond that, relatively little is known about the early settlers. It bears noting that Holland at that time was a very prosperous and desirable place to live. As a result, few Dutch people had any incentive to cross the ocean. Rather, those who came to New Amsterdam were people of many different nationalities who were searching for economic opportunities. From its inception then, the town that would one day become New York was a melting pot.
	In the countryside, outside of New Amsterdam, the situation was markedly different. Intent on consolidating their control of the area, the Dutch instituted a system of "patroonships." Anyone who could finance the settlement of 50 adults was named a "patroon," or landowner, and was granted large parcels of land and feudal rights. Land ownership was denied to common workers, who had little choice but to labor on the land of their patroons. In many ways, this system bears a striking resemblance to Europe in the Middle Ages, with large blocks of land and exclusive political power centered in the hands of a very few.

Understandably, the colony's governors, whose role it was to implement and maintain this system, were unpopular with the people and got little support from them. Given the climate in which they lived, it's perhaps not surprising that when the British soldiers arrived in the harbor of New Amsterdam prepared for battle, the Dutch settlers surrendered to them without a fight.

NARRATOR: Now get ready to answer the question.

NARRATOR: Using points and examples from the talk, explain the factors that contributed to the loss of Holland's colony of New Amsterdam.

WRITING SECTION

Task 1

Track 52

NARRATOR: Now listen to part of a talk on the topic you just read about.

PROFESSOR: As more and more companies have gone "global," there's been a huge increase in the number of employees based outside of the U.S. The trend is for companies to decentralize operations, making the move from manufacturing an entire TV, say, to focusing only on its core competencies … Maybe it manufactures just the TV screen rather than the complete TV, as it did 20 years ago.

This increased specialization results in companies taking their noncore operations and shipping them to some other country where skilled labor costs a fraction of what it does here in the U.S.

So what does this mean for the American working public? By taking various operations—including sales and customer service—away from the U.S., companies are flat out removing jobs from our economy. As larger companies shift their information technology services, call centers, and other operations to cheaper jurisdictions, everyone performing those functions here in the U.S. loses their jobs. Generally, working class people lose their jobs while upper management remains untouched. In some cases, yes, outsourcing makes a company more profitable, which should benefit employees in the long run, but more often than not, just results in lost jobs.

Outsourcing is a fact of life, and we can't escape it. The only way we can help protect American jobs is by encouraging companies to educate the workers whose jobs are moving offshore. If companies commit to building the skill sets and experience of workers here in the U.S., there's a chance that they'll also award these employees with better-paying positions once their current jobs are outsourced. If that happens, outsourcing will be a win-win situation for everyone involved.

Narrator: Summarize the points made in the lecture you just heard, and then compare the speaker's opinion with the opinion stated in the reading.

Answers and Explanations

PRACTICE TEST 1

Reading Section

Passage 1: Nathaniel Hawthorne: His Life and Work

1 (D)
2 (A)
3 (C)
4 (B)
5 (B)
6 (A)
7 (C)
8 (C)
9 (B)
10 (B)
11 (A)
12 (C)
13 *The Scarlet Letter*: (A), (C), (F), (H); *The House of the Seven Gables*: (B), (E), (G)

Passage 2: The Biological Effects of Ionizing Radiation

14 (B)
15 (D)
16 (A)
17 (B)
18 (A)
19 (A)
20 (D)
21 (D)
22 (C)
23 (B)
24 (C)
25 (A), (C), (D)

Passage 3: The Social Cognitive Theory of Learning

26 (C)
27 (A)
28 (B)
29 (C)
30 (D)
31 (A)
32 (A)
33 (C)
34 (B)
35 (A)
36 (D)
37 (A)
38 (A), (B), (E)

Listening Section

Dialogue 1

1 (C)
2 (D)
3 (A)
4 (D)
5 (B)

Dialogue 2

6 (C)
7 (A)
8 (C)
9 (B)
10 (C)

Academic Talk 1: Art History

11 (C)
12 (A)
13 (B), (C)
14 (C)
15 (A)
16 (A)

Academic Talk 2: Archaeology

17 (D)
18 (C)
19 (C)
20 (B)
21 (A)
22 *yes:* (A), (D), (E); *no:* (B), (C)

Academic Talk 3: History

23 (B)

24 (C)

25 (D)

26 (C)

27 (A)

28 (A), (B), (D)

Academic Talk 4: Literature

29 (B)

30 (A)

31 (A)

32 (D)

33 (C)

34 (B)

Speaking Section

1 Answers will vary. **Skill tested:** Describe based on a familiar experience

2 Answers will vary. **Skill tested:** Express and support an opinion based on a familiar experience

3 Answers will vary. **Skill tested:** Summarize and compare information gleaned from multiple sources

4 Answers will vary. **Skill tested:** Summarize and compare information gleaned from multiple sources

5 Answers will vary. **Skill tested:** Summarize main points and express and support an opinion

6 Answers will vary. **Skill tested:** Summarize and compare information gleaned from a lecture

Writing Section

1 Answers will vary. **Skill tested:** Summarize and compare information gleaned from multiple sources

2 Answers will vary. **Skill tested:** Express and support an opinion based on a familiar experience

PRACTICE TEST 2

Reading Section

Passage 1: How Satellites Have Revolutionized Communication

1 (A)

2 (B)

3 (A)

4 (B)

5 (A)

6 (A)

7 (C)

8 (D)

9 (A)

10 (C)

11 (B)

12 (A), (C), (D)

Passage 2: Alexander Hamilton: America's Visionary Economist

13 (C)

14 (B)

15 (D)

16 (D)

17 (C)

18 (A)

19 (A)

20 (D)

21 (B)

22 (A)

23 (B), (C), (E)

Passage 3: The Incandescent Lightbulb

24 (B)

25 (A)

26 (B)

27 (B)

28 (C)

29 (C)

30 (C)

31 (A)

32 (D)

33 (D)

34 (A)

35 (D)

36 *Incandescent bulbs*: (A), (D), (F), (I); *Fluorescent bulbs*: (C), (E), (H)

Listening Section

Dialogue 1

1 (B)

2 (D)

3 (D)

4 (C)

5 (A)

Dialogue 2

6 (A)

7 (B)

8 (D)

9 (A)

10 (B)

Academic Talk 1: Music

11 (B)

12 (A)

13 (C)

14 (D)

15 (C)

16 (B), (C), (D)

Academic Talk 2: Film History

17 (C)

18 (A)

19 (B)

20 (D)

21 (C)

22 (A), (D)

Academic Talk 3: History

23 (A)

24 (C)

25 (B)

26 (A)

27 (A)

28 (A)

Academic Talk 4: Physics

29 (D)

30 (C)

31 (A)

32 (A)

33 (B)

34 (B), (C), (D)

Speaking Section

1 Answers will vary. **Skill tested:** Describe based on a familiar experience

2 Answers will vary. **Skill tested:** Express and support an opinion based on a familiar experience

3 Answers will vary. **Skill tested:** Summarize and compare information gleaned from multiple sources

4 Answers will vary. **Skill tested:** Summarize and compare information gleaned from multiple sources

5 Answers will vary. **Skill tested:** Summarize main points and express and support an opinion

6 Answers will vary. **Skill tested:** Summarize and compare information gleaned from a lecture

Writing Section

1 Answers will vary. **Skill tested:** Summarize and compare information gleaned from multiple sources

2 Answers will vary. **Skill tested:** Express and support opinion based on a familiar experiences.

PRACTICE TEST 3

Reading Section

Passage 1: Acid Rain

1 (C)
2 (D)
3 (A)
4 (A)
5 (C)
6 (A)
7 (B)
8 (A)
9 (D)
10 (B)
11 (B)
12 (B), (D), (F)

Passage 2: Samuel Adams and the Shot Heard Around the World

13 (C)
14 (C)
15 (A)
16 (B)
17 (D)
18 (B)
19 (D)
20 (B)
21 (A)
22 (A)
23 (A)
24 (D)
25 *Actions taken by the British*: (A), (D), (G);
   Actions taken by the colonists: (B), (E), (F), (I)

Passage 3: Attention Deficit/Hyperactivity Disorder

26 (A)
27 (A)
28 (D)

29 (B)
30 (B)
31 (C)
32 (B)
33 (D)
34 (C)
35 (B)
36 (C), (D), (E)

Listening Section

Dialogue 1

1 (D)
2 (C)
3 (B)
4 (A)
5 (C)

Dialogue 2

6 (D)
7 (B)
8 (C)
9 (A)
10 (A)

Academic Talk 1: Women's Studies

11 (A)
12 (C)
13 (B)
14 (D)
15 (B)
16 (A), (C), (D)

Academic Talk 2: Film Studies

17 (B)
18 (B), (C)
19 (A)
20 (B)
21 (B)
22 (C)

Academic Talk 3: Music

23 (C)

24 (D)

25 (A)

26 (C)

27 (D)

28 (A), (B), (C)

Academic Talk 4: History

29 (D)

30 (A)

31 (C)

32 (B)

33 (B)

34 (B)

Speaking Section

1 Answers will vary. **Skill tested:** Describe based on a familiar experience

2 Answers will vary. **Skill tested:** Express and support an opinion based on a familiar experience

3 Answers will vary. **Skill tested:** Summarize and compare information gleaned from multiple sources

4 Answers will vary. **Skill tested:** Summarize and compare information gleaned from multiple sources

5 Answers will vary. **Skill tested:** Summarize main points and express and support an opinion

6 Answers will vary. **Skill tested:** Summarize and compare information gleaned from a lecture

Writing Section

1 Answers will vary. **Skill tested:** Summarize and compare information gleaned from multiple sources

2 Answers will vary. **Skill tested:** Express and support an opinion based on a familiar experience

PRACTICE TEST 4

Reading Section

Passage 1: Hubble's "Tuning Fork" Galaxy Diagram

1 (B)

2 (D)

3 (B)

4 (B)

5 (D)

6 (C)

7 (A)

8 (A)

9 (D)

10 (D)

11 (A)

12 *Spiral galaxies*: (A), (D), (F); *Elliptical galaxies*: (B), (C), (G), (H)

Passage 2: Ellis Ruley, Folk artist

13 (C)

14 (A)

15 (B)

16 (A)

17 (A)

18 (A)

19 (D)

20 (A)

21 (A)

22 (C)

23 (A), (E), (F)

Passage 3: Nuclear Reactors

24 (A)

25 (D)

26 (A)

27 (C)

28 (A)

29 (D)

30 (C)

31 (B)

32 (B)

33 (C)

34 (A), (C), (F)

Listening Section

Dialogue 1

1 (C)

2 (B)

3 (B)

4 (A)

5 (D)

Dialogue 2

6 (B)

7 (B)

8 (C)

9 (A)

10 (D)

Academic Talk 1: Film Studies

11 (D)

12 (A), (C)

13 (C)

14 (A)

15 (B)

16 (A), (B), (D)

Academic Talk 2: Biology

17 (A)

18 (C)

19 (C)

20 (D)

21 (C)

22 (D)

Academic Talk 3: Film Studies

23 (A)

24 (C)

25 (B)

26 (B)

27 (C)

28 (A), (D), (E)

Academic Talk 4: Astronomy

29 (B)

30 (D)

31 (A)

32 (B)

33 (D)

34 (D)

Speaking Section

1 Answers will vary. **Skill tested:** Describe based on a familiar experience

2 Answers will vary. **Skill tested:** Express and support an opinion based on a familiar experience

3 Answers will vary. **Skill tested:** Summarize and compare information gleaned from multiple sources

4 Answers will vary. **Skill tested:** Summarize and compare information gleaned from multiple sources

5 Answers will vary. **Skill tested:** Summarize main points and express and support an opinion

6 Answers will vary. **Skill tested:** Summarize and compare information gleaned from a lecture

Writing Section

1 Answers will vary. **Skill tested:** Summarize and compare information gleaned from multiple sources

2 Answers will vary. **Skill tested:** Express and support an opinion based on a familiar experience